THE ECONOMICS OF PEACEMAKING
Focus on the Egyptian-Israeli Situation

This study, as its title implies, is about economic aspects of peacemaking. It was obviously inspired by the events leading to the signing of the Egyptian-Israeli Peace Treaty in March 1979. The book's primary concern, however, is not with the Middle East peace process or peace prospects; it has a more general perspective. The point of departure is that while every war and every peace are unique, certain aspects of the peacemaking process have common characteristics. It is with some of these characteristics, particularly the economic ones, that the book is concerned.

The book offers an economic interpretation of key concepts such as dependence and interdependence, which are crucial to the understanding of the relationship between economics and peacemaking. Interdependence is viewed as a state characterised by an acceptable balance between gains from economic transactions between recent or potential belligerents and losses from disruption caused by dissociation between them.

The discussion then turns to the consideration of the impact of different types of transactions on the economic welfare and vested interest in peace of different sectors of the population such as consumers and producers. Distinction is made between transactions which lead to the expansion of existing facilities and those involving the establishment of new activities which before peace were uneconomical because of factors such as high international transfer costs or economies of scale. Consideration is also given to the potential contribution of third parties to the economics of peacemaking. They can increase the volume and scope of cooperative ventures by offering missing ingredients such as supplies, know-how or markets. Moreover, their presence reduces the risks involved in dissociation by one of the recent belligerents.

The validity, usefulness and implications of these concepts are illustrated by case studies and detailed examples pertaining to the economies of the countries involved in the Middle East peace process.

THE ECONOMICS OF PEACEMAKING

Focus on the Egyptian-Israeli Situation

by

Ruth Arad
Seev Hirsch
and
Alfred Tovias

St. Martin's Press   New York

© Ruth Arad, Seev Hirsch and Alfred Tovias and the Trade Policy
Research Centre 1983

ISBN 0–312–23441–4

Library of Congress Cataloging in Publication Data

Arad, Ruth W.
  The economics of peacemaking.

  Bibliography: p.
  Includes index.
    1. Egypt—Foreign economic relations—Israel.
2. Israel—Foreign economic relations—Egypt.   3. Egypt—
Foreign relations—Israel.   4. Israel—Foreign relations
—Egypt.   I. Hirsch, Seev.   II. Tovias, Alfred.
III. Trade Policy Research Centre.   IV. Title.
HF3886.Z71752   1983   337.5694062   83–4569
ISBN 0–312–23441–4

Trade Policy Research Centre

issues. As a non-profit organisation, which is privately sponsored, the
institute has been developed to work on an international basis and serves as
an entrepreneurial centre for a variety of activities, ranging from the

227504

sponsorship of research, the organisation of meetings and a publications programme which includes a quarterly journal, *The World Economy*. In general, the Centre provides a focal point for those in business, the universities and public affairs who are interested in the problems of international economic relations – whether commercial, legal, financial, monetary or diplomatic.

The Centre is managed by a Council, set out above, which represents a wide range of international experience and expertise.

Publications are presented as professionally competent studies worthy of public consideration. The interpretations and conclusions in them are those of their respective authors and should not be attributed to the Council, staff or associates of the Centre which, having general terms of reference, does not represent a consensus of opinion on any particular issue.

Enquiries about membership (individual, corporate or library) of the Centre, about subscriptions to *The World Economy* or about the Centre's publications should be addressed to the Director, Trade Policy Research Centre, 1 Gough Square, London EC4A 3DE, United Kingdom, or to the Centre's Washington office, Suite 640, 1120 20th Street, N.W., Washington, D.C. 20036, United States of America.

Contents

Trade Policy Research Centre v
List of Tables x
List of Figures xi
Biographical Notes xii
Preface xiii
Introduction xv
Abbreviations xix

PART ONE
GENERAL ANALYSIS OF THE PEACEMAKING PROCESS

Chapter 1
PROCESS OF PEACEMAKING AND INTERDEPENDENCE 3
    What is the Economics of Peacemaking About? 3
    Balance of Terror and Balance of Prosperity 5
    Gains from International Transactions 7
    Interdependence and Related Concepts 10
    Notes and References 20

Chapter 2
INTERDEPENDENCE BETWEEN PAST BELLIGERENTS ......,........ 23
    Dependence 23
    Cost of Dissociation 26
    Interdependence 28
    Interdependence and Deterrence 34
    Maximising Expected Gains 37
    Risk of Dissociation 39
    Interdependence: a Dynamic Perspective 43

Notes and References 46

Chapter 3
PEACEMAKING, VESTED INTERESTS AND
INTERNATIONAL TRANSACTIONS 47
Vested Interest in Peace 47
Initiating Trade between Recent Belligerents 50
Export Diversion 55
Import Expansion and Export Expansion 56
Export Creation and Output Creation 59
Effect of Trade on Welfare and Vested Interest in Peace 61
Policy Implications 63
A Possible Example 66
Notes and References 68

Chapter 4
COOPERATIVE VENTURES BETWEEN
RECENT ENEMIES 71
Cooperative Ventures 71
Dominance 74
The Role of Third Parties 76
More on the Role of Third Parties 79
Conclusions 81
Notes and References 83

PART TWO
THE EGYPTIAN-ISRAELI PEACE PROCESS

Chapter 5
POTENTIAL TRADE BETWEEN EGYPT AND ISRAEL 87
Border Trade 89
A Linear Regression Model 94
Results of the Regression Model 97
Demand 98
Supply 99
Resistance Parameters 100
Potential Egyptian-Israeli Trade Patterns 103
Conclusions 115
Notes and References 115

Chapter 6
INSTITUTIONAL ARRANGEMENTS BETWEEN
  EGYPT AND ISRAEL 117
  Discrimination, Integration and Normalisation 118
  Trade Cooperation 121
  Advanced Forms of Integration 125
  Sectoral Approach: the ECSC 126
  Sectoral Approach: the Textiles and Clothing Sector 128
  Notes and References 132

Chapter 7
SHORT-TERM PERSPECTIVES ON ECONOMIC RELATIONS........ 135
  Political Considerations 135
  Nature of Bilateral Transactions 138
  Business Environment 139
  Arrangements Requiring International Cooperation 141
  Concluding Remarks 143
  Notes and References 145

Appendix 1
SELECTION OF EQUILIBRIUM LEVEL OF BILATERAL
  ECONOMIC TRANSACTIONS 147
Appendix 2
PARAMETERS ESTIMATED BY THE REGRESSION
  MODEL OF BORDER AND BILATERAL TRADE 149
Appendix 3
TEXT OF THE EGYPTIAN-ISRAELI AGREEMENT
  ON TRADE AND COMMERCE 157

Selected Bibliography 161

Index 167

List of Tables

2.1   Determination of Independence, Dependence and Interdependence (Symbolic Presentation) 32

2.2   Economic Gains, Costs of Dissociation and Expected Income (an Example) 38

3.1   Different Trade Effects and their Impact on Vested Interest in Peace 60

4.1   Characteristics of Trilateral Cooperative Ventures 78

5.1   Industries with the Highest and Lowest Border-trade Indices 93

5.2   Highest and Lowest Resistance to Trade Parameters 104

5.3   Diversion Potential 107

5.4   Diversion and Expansion Potential 108

5.5   High Expansion Potential 110

5.6   Ordinary Expansion Potential 111

5.7   Summary of Diversion Potential 113

5.8   Summary of Trade Potential 114

6.1   Egyptian and Israeli International Trade in Textiles and Clothing, 1979 130

A.1   Border-trade Shares for Six Categories 149

A.2   Normalised Border-trade Indices 151

A.3   Border-trade Indices 153

A.4   Summary of Results of Regression Parameters 154

List of Figures

2.1   Economic Gains and Dependence 25
2.2   A's National Product under Different Conditions 27
2.3   Determination of Independence, Dependence and
        Interdependence 30
2.4   Interdependence and Deterrence 35
3.1   Export Diversion, Increasing Costs 54
3.2   Export Diversion, Decreasing Costs 55
3.3   Import Expansion and Export Expansion,
        Increasing Costs 57
3.4   Import Expansion, Decreasing Costs 58
3.5   Export and Output Creation 59
5.1   Box Plots of Border-trade Figures 90

Biographical Notes

RUTH ARAD has been a Lecturer at the Leon Recanati Graduate School of Business Administration, Tel Aviv University, in Israel, since 1975. After serving in the Israeli Air Force, she graduated from Tel Aviv University and obtained her masters degree and doctorate at Princeton University in the United States, in the course of which she was an economist at Johnson & Johnson, New Jersey, and at the Morgan Guaranty Trust, New York. Dr Arad has contributed to a number of professional journals and written several monographs.

SEEV HIRSCH has been, since 1981, Mel and Sheila Jaffee Professor of International Trade at the Leon Recanati Graduate School of Business Administration, Tel Aviv University. He joined the staff of the Leon Recanati School in 1965, after obtaining his masters degree, then his doctorate, at the Harvard Graduate School of Business Administration in the United States. Awarded a Rockefeller fellowship, he was in 1974-5 a Visiting Professor at the University of Oxford, the University of Reading and the Stockholm School of Economics, then in 1976 was a Visiting Lecturer at the World Bank's Economic Development Institute in Washington. Professor Hirsch is the author of *Location of Industry and International Competitiveness* (1967), *The Export Performance of Six Manufacturing Industries: a Comparative Study of Denmark, Holland and Israel* (1971) and *Rich Man's, Poor Man's and Every Man's Goods* (1977).

ALFRED TOVIAS has been a Lecturer in International Relations at the Hebrew University, Jerusalem, in Israel, since 1979. Born in Barcelona, in Spain, he studied at the University there before transferring to the University of Geneva, in Switzerland, where he obtained his doctorate and later held teaching posts as Chef de Travaux and then Chargé de Cours. Dr Tovias is the author of *Théorie et Pratique des Accords Commerciaux Préférentiels* (1974) and, for the Trade Policy Research Centre, *Tariff Preferences in Mediterranean Diplomacy* (1977).

Preface

Reliance on markets, with private initiative bringing about adjustment, is the only way, consistent with the rights of the individual, to ensure peaceful and prosperous coexistence both within a society and between societies. Avoidance of discriminatory policies, within an economy and between economies, is therefore crucial and explains why in the late 1940s, following the autarkic and discriminatory policies of the 1930s, the architects of the international economic order established after World War II set so much store by the principle of non-discrimination.

Much of the work of the Trade Policy Research Centre has been concerned with what it takes to sustain a stable, and therefore durable, international economic order as the basis for the maintenance of peace and prosperity between nations. For the most part that work has dealt with issues in a global context.

This is the first study that the Trade Policy Research Centre has sponsored which is specifically concerned with the economics of *establishing* peace between recent belligerents. Ruth Arad, Seev Hirsch and Alfred Tovias devote a large part of their study to general issues in *The Economics of Peacemaking* before turning to the particular, and all too real, problems in the part of the world in which they live. They build on Albert O. Hirschman's classic work on *National Power and the Structure of Foreign Trade* and draw on the experience of the European Community in underpinning the Franco-German *rapprochement*. On the fragile peace between Egypt and Israel reached in the Camp David accords, they are too close to realities to indulge in any grand designs, focussing instead on feasible first steps on the path of *economic* integration – involving no more than the lowering of restrictions on the movement of goods and services and, possibly, the factors of production.

As usual, it has to be stressed that the views expressed in this study do not necessarily reflect the views of the Council or those of the staff and associates of the Trade Policy Research Centre which, having general terms of

reference, does not represent on any particular issue a consensus of opinion.
The purpose of the Centre is to promote independent analysis and public
discussion of international economic policy issues.

HUGH CORBET
Director
Trade Policy Research Centre

London
August 1982

Introduction

Economists tend to shy away from subjects such as economics of peacemaking, which by their very nature are untidy, emotion-laden and require an inter-disciplinary approach. While acknowledging the existence of these problems, we felt that the economics of peacemaking is a subject which is both empirically important and analytically interesting.

This book was obviously inspired by the Egyptian-Israeli Peace Treaty of March 1979. The book's primary concern, however, is not with the Middle East peace process or peace prospects; it has a more general perspective. The point of departure is that while every war and every peace are unique, certain aspects of the peacemaking process have common characteristics. It is with some of these characteristics, particularly the economic ones, that the book is concerned.

The first part of the book focusses on theory, offering a number of conceptual schemes or models which can be applied to the analysis of economic aspects of peacemaking. The second part is concerned with applications, prediction of trade patterns likely to emerge between recent belligerents and examination of alternative institutional frameworks suitable for the development of economic relations between them.

Part One contains four chapters. Chapter 1 discusses different interpretations of the term 'economics of peacemaking'. It analyses key concepts such as dependence and interdependence, which are crucial to the understanding of the relationship between economics and peacemaking, and traces their development in the political science and economics literature.

Interdependence is also dealt with in Chapter 2, which considers the question of optimal interdependence; that is, establishing an acceptable trade-off between economic gains from bilateral transactions between recent belligerents (or unfriendly nations) and political and economic dependence which such transactions inevitably bring about. A number of rigorous definitions amenable, at least in principle, to quantitative measurement and to systematic analysis of policy alternatives are offered and examined.

Chapter 3 focusses on the internal impact of economic transactions between recent belligerents. It distinguishes between different types of bilateral transactions and considers methods of assessing their impact on the welfare of different sectors of the population and on vested interest in peace.

Additional transactions, involving cooperative ventures between the past belligerents and transactions involving third parties are considered in Chapter 4. The analysis deals with the control of bilateral and trilateral ventures and considers in particular the role which third parties can play in the development of economic relations between recent belligerents, including the level of transactions and their composition.

The second part of the book is concerned with a specific peacemaking process – between Egypt and Israel. The Egyptian-Israeli peace is admittedly only the first step in the long and arduous search for a comprehensive peace settlement encompassing Israel, the Palestinians and the Arab states. Inevitably, economics will play a more important and more interesting role in the settlement of the Palestinian question than in the bilateral economic relations likely to emerge between Egypt and Israel.

Settlement of the Palestinian question, however, is not yet within sight. An economic analysis of such a settlement is premature, due to lack of information on its institutional and political framework. It was therefore decided to focus the empirical part of the book on economic relations between Egypt and Israel.

Part Two consists of three chapters. Chapter 5, which presents trade projections, is concerned with the identification of candidates for trade between Egypt and Israel. While actual projections pertain to this particular pair of countries, the methodology developed in the chapter is valid for other cases where trade between two parties is non-existent or where existing trade does not reflect the full potential.

Chapter 6 deals with alternative institutional frameworks for economic relations between Egypt and Israel, taking into account political constraints, differences in economic structure, industrialisation levels and other factors which are bound to affect the level, composition and type of bilateral economic relations between the two countries. A number of institutional arrangements, ranging from conventional trade agreements within the framework of the General Agreement on Tariffs and Trade (GATT) to comprehensive economic integration schemes, are examined in the chapter.

The last part of this chapter considers in some detail the possibilities and implications of partial integration covering a specific sector – textiles and clothing. The approach is inspired by the example of the European Coal and Steel Community (ECSC), established in the early 1950s, which constituted the first step in the economic integration between countries which, like Egypt and Israel, had been enemies for many years.

As long as an agreement on the Autonomy seems remote, Egypt and Israel are unlikely to enter into preferential agreements even if they offer substantial economic benefits to both countries. The concluding chapter deals therefore with the short run. Political and economic factors which influence the volume and composition of economic transactions are examined. The chapter concludes that even during this time frame investment-related trade and trade associated with transfer of know-how and technology are likely to account for a substantial share of economic transactions between Egypt and Israel.

As this book goes to press the Middle East is engulfed in yet another war. The Lebanese war, like the four Arab-Israeli wars which preceded it since the establishment of Israel in 1948, has few, if any, economic causes. Neither side can possibly expect to derive economic gains from it, whatever its outcome. If, however, a political solution can be found, then peace can be enhanced by economic means. Economics, while not being a cause of the conflict, might become, if properly handled, an instrument of reconciliation.

This book examines some of the problems involved in translating this apparently simple idea into reality, that is, into policies, projects and transactions. The Lebanese war demonstrates once again that the Arab-Israeli conflict cannot be solved by military means alone; neither side can realistically expect to achieve a total victory which will enable it to impose its will over the other.

If a solution is possible at all, it must be based on a mutually-acceptable compromise between Israel and her adversaries, amongst whom the Palestinians have come to occupy a major position.

Only after the guns fall silent can the economics of peacemaking be given their chance.

Some of the material contained in the book is based on papers published in academic journals. These include: Arad and Hirsch, 'Peacemaking and Vested Interests: International Economic Transactions', *International Studies Quarterly*, Beverly Hills, September 1981, pp. 439-67; Arad and Hirsch, 'Potential Trade Between Egypt and Israel', *Weltwirtschaftliches Archiv*, Kiel, vol. 118, no. 1, 1982, pp. 62-78.

Some passages in Chapter 7 were taken from Hirsch, 'Peace Making and Economic Interdependence', *The World Economy*, London, December 1981.

We are grateful for the comments and encouragement offered by Albert O. Hirschman, of the Institute of Advanced Study, Princeton University, who met with us shortly after we decided to engage in this endeavour. His book *National Power and the Structure of Foreign Trade*, first published in 1945, was very influential in shaping our approach. We also wish to thank Robert O. Keohane, of Brandeis University, Waltham, Massachusetts, for his comments and suggestions. His work (together with that of Joseph S. Nye, of Harvard University) on interdependence and their distinction between sensitivity and vulnerability interdependence have become basic concepts in the literature and have been useful in enriching our own thinking.

Thanks are due to numerous friends and colleagues from Tel Aviv University, the Hebrew University of Jerusalem and several other institutions in Israel, the United Kingdom, the United States and Switzerland, who read and commented on parts of the manuscript or papers on which the final manuscript is based.

Generous financial support was provided by Tel Aviv University through its Research Project on Peace, the Project for Joint Economic Development in the Middle East, the Samuel Rubin Research Fund in the Middle East and Developing Countries and the Israel Institute of Business Research.

Gerda Kessler assisted with the literature survey and with editing; she also typed the manuscript on that electronic marvel – the computerised word processor.

Finally, we wish to thank Theresa Hunt, Janet Strachan and Eri Nicolaides, of the Trade Policy Research Centre in London, for their role in getting the book into final shape.

In conclusion, we would like to express the hope that we shall soon have the chance to discuss our work with colleagues at the universities of Cairo, Amman, Bir Zeit and other Arab universities. There could be no more fitting tribute to the relevance of the economics of peacemaking.

RUTH ARAD
SEEV HIRSCH
ALFRED TOVIAS

Tel Aviv
August 1982

Abbreviations

CACM	Central American Common Market
c.i.f.	prices including cost, insurance and freight
Comecon	Council for Mutual Economic Assistance
EAC	East African Community
ECSC	European Coal and Steel Community
EFTA	European Free Trade Association
f.o.b.	free-on-board prices
GATT	General Agreement on Tariffs and Trade
GNP	gross national product
LAFTA	Latin American Free Trade Association
MFN	most-favoured-nation clause,expressing the principle of non-discrimination
OECD	Organisation for Economic Cooperation and Development
OPEC	Organisation of Petroleum Exporting Countries
SITC	Standard International Trade Classification
UNCTAD	United Nations Conference on Trade and Development

A General Analysis of the Peacemaking Process

CHAPTER 1

Process of Peacemaking and Interdependence

The term 'economics of peacemaking' can mean different things to different people. It could refer to the economic constraints faced by the belligerents and to the economic reasons which impel them to seek peace. It has indeed been suggested that Egypt's and Israel's economic predicament contributed to Anwar Sadat's and Prime Minister Menachem Begin's decision to move in the direction of peace. The economic burden of carrying on with the war had been enormous for both countries and the expectation of continuously mounting defence outlays was one of the factors which persuaded their leaders to seek a political resolution of their conflict.

WHAT IS THE ECONOMICS OF PEACEMAKING ABOUT?

Several studies published in recent years attempted to calculate the economic burden of the conflict between Israel and the Arab countries.[1] Whatever their estimates they probably represent an understatement of the true costs of the conflict. This is because, as economist and social scientist Kenneth E. Boulding, of the University of Colorado, Boulder, noted:

'The losses due to war are of two kinds. There is the highly visible destruction of life and of goods, of which we are highly aware. On the other hand are the unborn and the unmade, that is the human beings who do not come into existence because of the decline in birth rates due to war and the goods which are not made because of the resources absorbed by the war industry.'[2]

'Economics of peacemaking' could also pertain to the costs and benefits of different peace settlements. John Maynard Keynes took this approach. In his book *The Economic Consequences of the Peace*, he vehemently attacked the provisions of the Versailles Peace Treaty, claiming that Germany could not possibly afford to pay the reparations demanded by the Allies and that the Allies' insistence on unattainable goals would ultimately lead to the breakdown of the peace.[3]

3

Game theorists have occasionally dealt with problems which might legitimately come under the heading of 'economics of peacemaking'. The theory, developed mostly by mathematicians and statisticians, is used widely by economists, political scientists, psychologists and other social scientists to study conflict situations. Game-theoretic models such as the Prisoner's Dilemma are concerned with situations where a pair of players who distrust each other choose outcomes which are clearly not optimal for either. If only they could bring themselves to cooperate, or if they could devise a mechanism which would insure one against being cheated by the other, both could be better off. The implications of these models for arms control and for other situations involving unfriendly nations are obvious.[4]

Professor Boulding, who dealt extensively with the economics of war and peace, used economic models to analyse problems of defence, armaments and the stabilisation of peace. Another important contribution of his is the interesting analytical distinction between the three systems which govern human affairs – the threat system, the exchange system and the integrative system.[5] The threat system, which dominates international relations and other aspects of human life, is characterised by reliance on force. The major premise of the threat system is that it is the fear of the damage they will suffer if they fail to respond favourably to the demands of the opposite party which impels persons, nations or groups to act.

The exchange system characterises economic relations on the inter-personal, inter-group, inter-firm and international levels. Unlike the threat system, under which people trade in 'bads', the exchange system is typified by trade in goods.

Finally, the integrative system pertains to relationships between people regarding themselves as close to each other in some sense. It is manifested when Man regards others as extensions of his own being – members of the same family, club, party, religious community, co-workers, friends.

Professor Boulding regards the value of the three systems as being hierarchical: the exchange system is preferable to the threat system and the integrative system is preferred to both. Progress, according to Professor Boulding, is manifested by reducing the role played by the lower order systems and increasing that of the higher order ones in inter-personal relations, in the life of nations and in international relations. Peacemaking in Professor Boulding's world implies moving from the threat system to the exchange system.

Our book seeks to pursue this theme. It focusses on the use of economics to bring about this transformation from one system into the other. 'Economics of peacemaking' in the present context should be viewed as the use of economic instruments, of economic policies and economic transactions to stabilise and to safeguard peace between recent or potential belligerents.

BALANCE OF TERROR AND BALANCE OF PROSPERITY

Can economic transactions, which by definition belong to the exchange system, be used as instruments in achieving the transition from one system to the other? In answering this question it may be useful to re-phrase it in terms borrowed from the world of the threat system.

Consider the familiar term 'balance of terror': a situation where a potential aggressor refrains from using force against the intended victim because of the relatively high probability of great destruction and loss of life which he will suffer. If both sides feel that way, peace (as the absence of active war) is preserved.

One can conceive of a theoretical positive equivalent of balance of terror, a 'balance of prosperity', namely a situation where the relatively certain benefits of bilateral cooperation between past (and potential) belligerents is enormous and where the realisation of these benefits is conditional upon their continued cooperation. If one side stops cooperating, not only will the other side suffer; the offender, too, will suffer substantial losses. If these losses are unacceptable, peace is secured.

If feasible, the balance-of-prosperity scheme would appear to be superior. It achieves the same results, to wit peace, while allowing both sides to benefit from a higher income. The idea is not new. Its superiority over the balance-of-terror alternative is self-evident. Yet it is rarely applied. The reason lies in the difficulty of achieving an arrangement based on the balance of prosperity which would be as credible as one based on the balance of terror.

Consider, for instance, the following example, a proposal made by Professor J. Rom, a Member of the *Knesset* (Israel's parliament), shortly after President Sadat's visit to Jerusalem in 1977. This example may well illustrate the difficulties in achieving non-belligerency by creating conditions for a balance of prosperity. Professor Rom suggested that Israel and Egypt, with the active participation of the United States, should jointly build one or more nuclear power stations in the Sinai. These stations were to supply both countries with much-needed electricity-generating power. Implicit in the proposal was the idea that neither Egypt nor Israel alone could benefit from this source of electricity. Supply would presumably be discontinued if either side failed to honour its commitments to cooperate with the other.

There is considerable appeal and even irony in this modern version of beating one's swords into ploughshares, since nuclear power can be used to enhance either the balance of terror or the balance of prosperity. But the practical question is whether the Sinai nuclear power scheme can give Israel and Egypt the same security as that presumably provided by their armed forces.

To answer this question it is necessary to consider what would happen if the scheme were applied and then one side tried to break the peace. In principle, physical aggression would be unthinkable, for both countries would consequently be plunged into total darkness in a modern version of the ninth plague described in the Book of Exodus. In today's version of this event, the power stations will cease functioning automatically and industry will come to a standstill; homes would be deprived of electricity, petrol stations would be unable to dispense fuel and the two nations would be immobilised within hours. Such prospects should deter the potential aggressor and induce it to seek alternative means for settling its disagreements with the other party.

It is easy to demonstrate, however, that this desirable outcome is by no means assured by the mere existence of the joint nuclear station. Both countries presumably have additional power stations which can supply their national grids and which might well take care of emergency needs. Unless all alternative sources of supply are dispensed with, the joint project could actually become a trap for the country which happens to be more dependent on it. That country could be blackmailed by the less dependent one because the former would suffer worse damage than the latter. The blackmail need not be political. It could be economic. It need not even be explicit. It could be implied.

Total, all-inclusive dependence (in the above case, dependence on a single source of electricity) could deter aggression. Insistence on it, however, makes no economic sense: the costs of a 'genuine' power failure or alternatively the nightmare of a 'genuine' labour dispute if both countries are to depend on a single joint source of power are simply intolerable. This example illustrates the difficulties of devising a voluntary economic mechanism, based on bilateral cooperation, which could serve as a substitute for adequate defence arrangements.

The most important difference between the balance of terror and the balance of prosperity lies in the fact that the balance of terror is established by (sequential) unilateral decisions. Each party acquires the desired capacity to inflict damage on the other through its own decisions. They may come in response to the other country's actions, but that response is determined independently. Balance of prosperity, by contrast, cannot be decided upon unilaterally, since no economic transaction can, by definition, be unilateral. Each transaction involves at least two parties and both must agree on the transaction and its terms before it can materialise. An explicit agreement on balance of prosperity implies giving up some sovereignty. It requires a very high degree of mutual trust and many mutually acceptable institutions capable of making rules, establishing prices and adjudicating conflicts in an acceptable manner. Such institutions can function, if at all, within states, but not internationally, and certainly not between recent enemies whose conflict has not yet been fully resolved. It is for these reasons that, while the idea of balance of prosperity is very attractive, its realisation in any specific situation, international politics being what they still are, is inordinately difficult if possible at all.

Nevertheless, economic transactions can play an important role in stabilising peace between recent belligerents, provided they are properly handled. Otherwise, they can have counter-productive and destabilising effects, which can be disastrous if peace itself is fragile. Simply put, the peace-enhancing effects of economic transactions can be derived from the increase in the well being of both parties made possible by bilateral transactions.

GAINS FROM INTERNATIONAL TRANSACTIONS

International trade and investments create important economic benefits for those involved. In the absence of trade, residents of a given country would not have access to natural resources unavailable domestically and they would have to pay high prices for goods they could not produce efficiently. Thus Japan's status as a major industrial power would be very much reduced if her industry had to be powered by domestic energy. Saudi Arabia and Kuwait would remain in economic misery if they could not export their oil and exchange it for the goods and services they import in such abundance.

Moreover, international trade theory shows that the benefits from trade go way beyond the satisfaction derived from the barter of natural resources or resource-based goods. Additional gains are derived from specialisation. When trade is possible, countries do not produce all the goods which they are technically capable of producing. They gain more by limiting production to those goods in the production of which they are most efficient. Output of these exceeds local consumption and the surplus is exported in exchange for goods in which they are least efficient. Each country can thus consume the full range of goods which it can afford to buy, regardless of whether these goods are produced domestically or abroad.

Trade is particularly important for the economies of small countries. In the first place, a smaller range of natural resources is likely to be found within the borders of a small country. Both the United States and the Soviet Union have huge deposits of raw materials within their boundaries. Their land mass is so large as to have both tropical and arctic climates; it is large enough in each case to provide the manpower, infra-structure, ancillary services and capital needed to support numerous industries characterised by economies of scale. By contrast, Switzerland, with her small physical size and population, produces a more limited range of goods. Yet she consumes the same variety of goods as the United States.

The benefits from international exchange are not limited to trade in goods. Services, too, can be traded internationally. Thus Scandinavian tourists flock to the Mediterranean to enjoy the beaches and sunshine in such short supply at home; and the City of London earns handsome profits from the provision of financial services and by operating efficient commodity markets.

Very substantial gains are also derived from the international transfer of proprietary knowledge. Technical knowledge, market knowledge and managerial skills are transferred across national borders in the form of direct investment by multinational enterprises, licensing agreements, the sale of turn-key projects or know-how agreements.

Increasingly, classical factors of production such as capital and labour are also entering into international transactions. Capital is transferred internationally in the form of short-term and long-term loans and acquisition of shares, as well as the direct investments mentioned above. Labour, too, is becoming increasingly mobile across international borders. There is little doubt that West Germany's car and steel industries would have been far less competitive internationally had it not been for the *Gastarbeiter* employed by that country's industries.

Since international economic transactions bring such obvious gains to the parties involved, they might also be used as an instrument in strengthening peace and, too, as an additional inducement to peacemaking. Indeed, in his entry on 'Peace' in the *International Encyclopedia of the Social Sciences*, Johan Galtung, of the Institute of Development Studies, University of Geneva, has the following to say:

'Some models of peace are based on interdependence between nations. Interdependence, or interaction where some kind of positive value is exchanged between the parties to the interaction, may vary in frequency (how often), volume (how much is transferred), and scope (variety of value exchanged). Trade between two nations is a good example of how all three can vary independently.'[6]

The proposition that economic transactions between recent belligerents will increase their well being is not self-evident. At first glance it appears that two small countries, even when they are neighbours, have little to gain from bilateral economic transactions such as trade in goods and services, investments and the movement of production factors such as labour, capital, technology and management. If the two countries have intensive economic relations with the rest of the world before peace, their economies are in fact partly integrated, even though they do not deal with each other directly. This is true, however, only in a world where transportation and other transfer costs are negligible and where economies of scale do not matter.

In fact, these two factors are very important, as evidenced by the high proportion of so-called border trade in the commerce of many countries, especially small ones. The bulk of international trade in perishables takes place between neighbouring countries, as does the trade in building materials and even in the more sophisticated service-intensive goods.

When border trade is not feasible, the size of a small domestic market does not often justify the establishment of even a single manufacturing plant capable of manufacturing at internationally competitive unit costs. When transportation and other transfer costs are high, the market is supplied by either high-cost imports (high because of the transfer costs) or by high-cost local products (high because of the inability to exploit economies of scale).

The economics of production and distribution could in some of these cases change drastically when trade with a neighbouring country, formerly interrupted by war, becomes feasible. Peace can thus be shown to extend the range of the tradeable sector – that is, the sector which produces goods and services which can be internationally traded.

Additional economic benefits for both parties can often be derived from joint infra-structure development: transportation facilities such as roads, railways and ports; communication facilities; joint power generation; joint handling of ecological problems and so on.

Such transactions can undoubtedly increase economic welfare in both countries. If cooperation increases the well being of those who cooperate this, in turn, should provide an additional incentive for peace keeping and should therefore have a stabilising effect on the peace process. Bilateral transactions, however, do have destabilising effects which ought to be recognised.

These destabilising effects can be caused by the fact that, while total welfare is enhanced by bilateral transactions, there are inevitable conflicts over the distribution of these gains, since in many cases there is no impartial judge who can equitably distribute costs and gains between the two parties. These destabilising effects are best understood when considered within the more general context of establishing economic relations between recent belligerents.

Consider two countries, A and B, which after many years of war decide to make peace and to establish economic relations with each other. A and B differ from other pairs of countries in several important respects. In all other countries, bilateral economic relations already exist and presumably form an established pattern. Changes in the volume, direction and composition of trade and investment do, of course, take place, but these tend to be marginal.[7] In the case of A and B, patterns of economic relations are non-existent; they need to be established.

The form, volume and composition of these relations are matters of legitimate concern to governments even in countries where business is conducted largely by the private sector. If, as claimed by Richard N. Cooper, of Harvard University, 'trade policy is foreign policy', this is even more true in the case of past belligerents seeking to stabilise a recently-won peace settlement.[8] The shape of bilateral economic relations will affect the degree of mutual involvement and of mutual dependence.

A and B have renounced war. This does not mean, however, that all issues between them are resolved and that rivalry exists no more. One assumes, nevertheless, that having concluded peace between them the contemplation of economic intercourse does not emanate from a desire to continue their conflict, albeit through economic rather than military means. After all, we are not concerned here with a deliberate effort at engaging in economic warfare, which is a totally different matter. Instead the governments of A and B actually seek to contain their political rivalry and develop bilateral economic relations based on an acceptable compromise between the gains available from transactions with the past enemy and the negative impact of the conflicts over their distribution and of dependence, which are both inevitable by-products of international economic transactions.

INTERDEPENDENCE AND RELATED CONCEPTS

The concepts of dependence, interdependence, dependency and autonomy as descriptions of economic and political relations between countries have been widely discussed in the post-World War II literature, especially, although not exclusively, in respect to the relations between developing and industrialised economies.

The term interdependence, however, was first introduced much earlier, in the eighteenth century, during the Enlightenment period in Europe, when it represented the rejection of the entire system of domestic governance and international politics associated with the nation state of the Westphalia era.[9]

Montesquieu, a leading philosopher of the Enlightenment period, introduced the main assumption concerning interdependence and its societal effect:

'The natural effect of commerce is to bring about peace. Two nations which trade together render themselves reciprocally dependent if the one has an interest in buying, the other has an interest in selling, and all unions are based on mutual needs.'[10]

This classical formulation has been branded as Utopian by twentieth-century writers such as Edward Hallett Carr, the noted historian of Trinity College, Cambridge.

'The Utopian assumption that there is a world interest in peace which is identifiable with the interest of each individual nation helped politicians and political writers everywhere to evade the unpalatable fact of a fundamental divergence of interests between nations.'[11]

Worse still, as critics of the premise concerning the alleged benefits of interdependence came to argue, notions of interdependence may be little more than 'the unconscious reflections of national policy based on a particular interpretation of national interest at a particular time ... [and] transparent disguises of selfish vested interest'.[12]

It is, nevertheless, a fact that since World War II interdependence has increased, especially in the industrialised West, although it might be argued that this has been caused more by the East-West split and the dominant role played by the United States in the international arena than by an inherent harmony of interests. Whether the degree and scope of international interdependence is on the rise, as compared with nineteenth-century Europe, may be debated, but this is irrelevant for, undoubtedly, interdependence today is global in scope and in many ways more complex than ever. It is therefore a characteristic feature of the modern world.

The traditional view was that military power dominated other forms of influence and that states in possession of military power controlled world affairs. It is apparent, however, that resources which endow nations with power capabilities have become more complex in the post-World War II era. In his reaction to the events of the early 1970s, Hans J. Morgenthau, author of the leading 'realist' text on international politics,[13] went so far as to announce an historically unprecedented severing of the functional relationship between political, military and economic power, shown in the possession by militarily weak countries of 'monopolistic or quasi-monopolistic control of raw materials essential to the operation of advanced economies'.[14]

Post-World War II theories of world politics have consistently portrayed a potential 'state of war' in which the behaviour of states is dominated by the constant danger of military conflict. This conception, labelled 'political realism', has been almost simultaneously challenged by the 'modernist' school, which sees telecommunications and jet travel as creating a 'global village' and believes that ever-growing, complex and interdependent social and economic transactions are creating what Lester R. Brown, senior fellow at the Overseas Development Council in Washington, D.C., and a leading authority on the world food problem, calls a 'world without borders'.[15] A number of scholars see our era as one in which the territorial state, which has been dominant in world politics for the four centuries since feudal times ended, is being eclipsed by non-territorial actors such as multinational enterprises, transnational social movements and international organisations. 'The state is about through as an economic unit', in the opinion of Charles P. Kindleberger, of the Massachusetts Institute of Technology.[16]

Robert O. Keohane, of Brandeis University, and Joseph S. Nye, of Harvard University, in their book *Power and Interdependence* give a concise statement of the traditionalists' dismissal of these modernist assertions.[17] The traditionalists, they say,

'... point to the continuity in world politics. Military interdependence has always existed and military power is still important in world politics – witness nuclear deterrence; the Vietnam, Middle East, and India-Pakistan wars; and Soviet influence in Eastern Europe or American influence in the Caribbean. Moreover, as the Soviet Union has shown, authoritarian states can, to a considerable extent, control telecommunications and social transactions that they consider disruptive. Even poor and weak countries have been able to nationalize multinational corporations, and the prevalence of nationalism casts doubt on the proposition that the nation state is fading away.'

The clash between two opposing historical forces, one pushing for more comprehensive international organisation and the other towards smaller sovereign political units, was foreseen by Professor Carr, who saw the future dilemma of the international system as one of striking a balance between self-determination and political independence, on the one hand, and the economic, technological and military dependence of these sovereign states on each other, on the other hand.[18] The trend towards the creation of compact and politically sovereign units, set in motion by the peace settlement of World War I, continues to this day. While the drafters of the post-World War I settlement were aware of the dangers of unbridled military power and sought to check this with a collective security scheme, they were unresponsive to an equally serious problem, namely that 'the self-determination of small nations was incompatible with unbridled economic power and complete economic interdependence'. [19] Professor Carr predicted that the tension created by the simultaneous processes of political self-determination and growing economic interdependence would be resolved by the bifurcation of political and economic organisation. The dismantling of the colonial empires and the demand for national independence assured the creation of more sovereign political units, just as the lack of self-sufficiency and presence of technological interdependence demanded the creation of multinational economic blocs, such as the European Community, the Council for Mutual Economic Assistance (Comecon) in Eastern Europe, the Latin American Free Trade Association (LAFTA) and the Central American Common Market (CACM).

The question that inevitably arises is how much global involvement should a state foster and how much vulnerability and loss of autonomy is a state willing to suffer?

In developing a coherent theoretical framework for the political analysis of interdependence, Professors Keohane and Nye in their book *Power and Interdependence* take upon themselves the task of 'distilling and blending the wisdom in the traditional, classic realist and the modernist world-without-borders views of world politics'.[20] In their thinking, international conflict does not disappear when interdependence prevails. On the contrary, the authors claim, conflicts take new forms and may even increase. At the same time, the traditional approaches to understanding conflict in world politics do not explain interdependence conflict. Applying the wrong image and wrong rhetoric to problems often leads to erroneous analysis and bad policy.

Interdependence, as reciprocal effects among countries or among actors in different countries, must be distinguished from inter-connectedness, according to Professors Keohane and Nye. Wherever there are reciprocal, although not necessarily symmetrical, costly effects of transactions there is interdependence. Where interactions do not imply significant costly effects, there is simply inter-connectedness.

It is evident *prima facie* that a country which has to import all of its petroleum requirements is likely to be more dependent on other countries for an uninterrupted flow of petroleum than a country that merely imports luxury goods. Moreover, costly effects may sometimes be directly and intentionally incurred by one of the parties, as happens in the Soviet-American strategic relationship. In other instances, they may be indirect or even unintentional: for example, collective action may be necessary to prevent disaster for an alliance whose members are interdependent, for an international economic system which may face chaos because of the absence of coordination or for an ecological system threatened by a gradual increase of industrial effluents.

The term interdependence is not limited to situations of mutual benefit. Interdependent relationships will always involve costs. The ensuing loss of autonomy is a case in point. In fact, more than one author has found the trade-off between interdependence and national sovereignty to be the politically most meaningful cost.[21] Yet it is impossible to specify *a priori* whether the benefits of a relationship will exceed the costs. Analysing costs and benefits of an interdependent relationship has two aspects: (i) joint gains or losses and (ii) relative gains and distribution. It should be borne in mind that joint gains do not obviate distributional conflict.

Interdependence, furthermore, must not be defined entirely in terms of situations of evenly balanced mutual dependence. It is the asymmetries in dependence that are most likely to provide sources of influence for actors in their dealings with one another. Evidently, less dependent actors can often use the interdependent relationship as a source of power in bargaining over an issue and also, perhaps, to affect other issues.

Professors Keohane and Nye make an important distinction between two types of interdependent relationships, sensitivity and vulnerability interdependence.[22]

Sensitivity interdependence is created by interaction within a set framework of policies. In terms of costs, sensitivity means liability to costly effects imposed from outside before policies are altered to try to change the situation. For example, the United States is less sensitive to oil-price rises than Japan, since it imports a smaller proportion of its petroleum requirements.

Vulnerability interdependence rests on the relative availability and costliness of the alternative policies that various actors face following imposition of an outside effect. It includes the strategic dimension that sensitivity interdependence omits. For example, two countries may be equally sensitive to a rise in petroleum prices, but the less vulnerable one will be that which finds the less costly alternative. Vulnerability focusses on which actors set the rules of the game. If one actor can reduce its costs by altering its policy, either domestically or internationally, sensitivity patterns will not be good indicators of its power sources.

Thus influence deriving from favourable asymmetries in sensitivity is very limited when the underlying asymmetries in vulnerability are unfavourable. Professors Keohane and Nye speak of a hierarchy in terms of dominance and cost of three types of asymmetrical interdependence: in descending order these are (i) military, (ii) non-military vulnerability and (iii) non-military sensitivity.[23]

In the last decade the debate on dependence (used in the general sense) has moved beyond the Latin American countries, where it mostly began, to Western Europe and the United States, from problems of dependent, non-autonomous development, stressed by Latin American scholars, to small-state difficulties in autonomously achieving national goals and to interdependence and dependence of advanced industrial economies. The focus has shifted from one of exclusive preoccupation with North-South problems to a much more varied inquiry in which North-South relations are supplemented by an examination of relations among industrialised countries, among developing countries and among producer organisations such as the Organisation of Petroleum Exporting Countries (OPEC) and regional actors such as the European Community.

In his introduction to a special issue of the journal *International Organization* on dependence and dependency in the global system, James A. Caporaso, Professor of Government at the Graduate School of International Studies of Denver University, applied the concept of 'asymmetric international relations' in relating to the areas of small-state and client-state behaviour, dominance and dependence, imperialism and great power-small power behaviour.[24] The inequality in the interactions or transactions among actors implied by the term covers unequal exchanges (as in terms of trade), power inequalities (as in the unequal abilities of actors to achieve compliance with their wishes) and structural inequalities in the more or less permanent relations among actors (for example, in the distribution of opportunities and constraints that impinge on each actor) and disregards differences in factors such as national literacy, wealth or development.

In another article on 'Dependence, Dependency, and Power in the Global System: a Structural and Behavioral Analysis', Professor Caporaso takes the general concept of 'dependence' and sub-divides it into 'dependence' and 'dependency', relating these concepts to 'interdependence' and autonomy.[25] He was prompted to do this by what he felt was the use of the term dependence to cover different concepts. Both dependence and dependency have predominant foci on relational inequalities among actors and both are equally interested in the vulnerabilities of the members of the global system resulting from the unequal relations.

Professor Caporaso uses the term dependence in the familiar common-sense manner to denote external reliance on other actors or an imbalance in relations between actors. Any country may be dependent on any other, through trade, technology transfer or cultural relations. When the exchanges, flows and transfers bringing about the provisions of needs are roughly symmetric, in Professor Caporaso's view, the relationship is one of interdependence. Thus dependence may simply be viewed as a highly asymmetric form of interdependence, which suggests mutual control. The dependence orientation seeks to probe and explore the symmetries and asymmetries among individual actors which are usually internally unified nation states confronting the external environment as homogeneous units. The conceptual components of dependence are the extent of one's reliance on another, the importance attached to the goods involved and the availability of these goods (or substitutes) from different sources. Dependence, as asymmetric interdependence, is a dyadic and a 'net' concept; that is, it is measured by gauging the difference between A's reliance on B and B's reliance on A. With the nation state as the basic unit of analysis, analysis of dependent relations can be carried out on any combination of states from dyads up to large groupings. The fact that dependence is a term that can be discussed meaningfully at the dyadic level allows one the luxury of dealing with a large number of observations. Thus dependence theory can easily be linked to statistical modes of analysis.

The term 'dependency', or 'dependencia theory', was developed in the early 1960s by scholars of the Third World's international relations who were critical of some of the alleged consequences of global domination by developed capitalist metropoles. The dependencia theory stresses that dependency is both a worldwide and historical phenomenon associated with the origins of capitalism and the emergence of the international division of labour. The dependency orientation seeks to explore the process of integration of the peripheral developing countries into the international capitalist system and the developmental implications of this peripheral capitalism.

The concept of dependency, according to Professor Caporaso, requires that we look at a unit in relation to all external influences. The focus is on (i) the class structure in the peripheral country, (ii) the alliance between this class structure and international capital and (iii) the role of the state in shaping and managing the national, foreign and class forces that propel development within countries. There is rarely, if ever, an attempt to identify the reciprocal dependencies of relevant external actors on the dependent country. Rather the dependencies are presumed to be so small as to justify treating them as non-existent. The dependency framework explicitly rejects the unified state as an actor, as a useful conceptual building block of theory. The global system is not seen as a collection of nation states, but in terms of a large number of interacting roles, specialised positions and statuses. Unlike the dependence framework, dependency theory visualises dependent relations in such a way as to make it impossible to focus simply on a pair of actors.

Not the whole country, but a selected portion of it, is integrated into the international economic system in a particular way. The specialisation of tasks runs across and within many states. Dependency theory, therefore, cannot easily be coupled to statistical analysis.

Thus, according to Professor Caporaso, while the opposite of dependence is interdependence, or mutual control, the opposite of dependency is autonomy, self-control and complete independence from unwanted causal influences (perhaps involving policies of isolationism and autarky). The lack of integration of the various parts of the domestic economy of the dependent country due to the strong linkages between portions of the economy and foreign economies, the marginal status of displaced groups and the growing gap between élites and masses in the dependent country are all examples of 'structural distortions' (a term referring to the numerous ways in which the local economy is structured to meet the needs of the foreign sector) which reflect the dependent country's lack of autonomy under dependency, particularly but not solely with respect to development goals.

Sanjaya Lall, of the Institute of Economics and Statistics at the University of Oxford, has succintly expressed the perpetuating effect of the lack of autonomy on the structural distortions and the consequent negative effect on the dependent country's development:

'In the usage of the dependencia school ... dependence is meant to describe certain characteristics (economic as well as social and political) of the economy as a whole and is intended to trace certain processes which are causally linked to its underdevelopment and which are expected to adversely affect its development in the future.'[26]

It is impossible, according to Professor Caporaso, to reduce dependency to a single, unidimensional concept. Perhaps in its most elementary version, dependency can be expressed as a syndrome of related concepts (such as external penetration, ties between local and foreign capital, structural integration or disintegration of various parts of the economy).[27] He suggests, furthermore, that dependency is not a concept in a theory, but a synoptic term for a body of theory.[28]

The concept of dependence is more easily integrated into bargaining theory while dependency is more fruitfully applied to analysis of the structure of relations among societies.

In the following definitions or descriptions, 'dependence' is taken to relate to Professor Caporaso's 'dependency'.

'By dependence we mean a situation in which the economy of certain countries is conditioned by the development and expansion of another economy to which the former is subjected. The relation of interdependence between two or more economies, and between these and world trade, assumes the form of dependence when some countries (the dominant ones) can expand and be self-sustaining, while other countries (the dependent ones) can do this only as a reflection of that expansion, which can have either a positive or negative effect on their immediate development.'[29]

Here dependency is defined as a causal relationship, a functional relationship among economies resulting in unequal autonomous development possibilities.

'Economic dependence we may define as a lack of capacity to manipulate the operative elements of an economic system. Such a situation is characterized by an absence of interdependence between the economic functions of a system. This lack of interdependence implies that the system has no internal dynamic which would enable it to function as an independent, autonomous entity.'[30]

Here, in Professor Caporaso's view,[31] dependency is equated with a particular species of non-autonomy, springing from the lack of interdependence of domestic economic sectors, on the one hand, and their corresponding dependence on external economic activity, on the other. Dependency, then, has an internal anatomy manifesting itself in fragmentation and an external anatomy realised through its responsiveness to foreign economic activity.

Fernando H. Cardoso, of the Brazilian Centre for Analysis and Planning in São Paulo, most clearly expresses dependency as a 'functional derangement' or 'functional incompleteness' of a national economy.

'Capitalist accumulation in dependent economies does not complete its cycle. Lacking "autonomous technology" – as vulgar parlance has it – and compelled therefore to utilize imported technology, dependent capitalism is crippled ... It is crippled because it lacks a fully developed capital goods sector. The accumulation, expansion, and self-realization of local capital requires and depends on a dynamic complement outside itself: it must insert itself into a circuit of international capitalism.'[32]

Dependency, in Professor Caporaso's view,[33] now becomes something more critical and more complex than a simple reliance on others for provision of goods. The concept of reliance remains critical, but it is reliance on external (or transnational) agencies for completion of basic economic activities.

The dependencia school is concerned with the effects of close economic ties between the periphery and the centre on the economic structure, income distribution and political development of the former. These effects might be regarded as indirect. The centre is not an actor with stated objectives and policies. Dependent development is the outcome or even inadvertent outcome of the sum total of influences derived from a multitude of individual uncoordinated transactions.

Another kind of dependence results from deliberate steps taken by national governments seeking to establish relationships of influence or even subordination with other national entities.

Professor Hirschman offers in his authoritative text, *National Power and the Structure of Foreign Trade*, a most interesting analysis of how economic measures can be used to gain political ends by means of power policy.

'A country trying to make the most out of its strategic position with respect to its own trade will try precisely to create conditions which make the interruption of trade of much graver concern to its trading partner than to itself. Tariff wars and interruption of trade rarely occur, but the awareness of their possibility is sufficient to test the influence of the stronger country and to shape the policy of the weaker.'[34]

Professor Hirschman illustrates this approach by describing the use of economic power by Nazi Germany to induce smaller states, especially the Balkans, to align themselves politically with the Axis camp. Germany offered preferential trade arrangements to these countries at a time when protectionism made access to international markets extremely difficult. Wide sectors in the victim countries became dependent on the German markets for their economic well being. In time it became evident to the leaders of these countries that failure to support the Axis politically would result in severe economic hardship. One of the conclusions which follow from this experience is that geographic diversification of markets not only makes good economic sense but also can be politically desirable.

In an interesting article published in 1978, Professor Hirschman acknowledged a shortcoming of his book, maintaining that modern dependency theory suffers from the same shortcoming: neither takes up the issue of the countervailing forces generated by the asymmetrical relations.[35] Both he and the dependency-school theorists had initially ignored two important factors. The first is the desire of the weaker dependent state for freedom from domination, which may be more powerful than the stronger power's desire to dominate. The second is the imbalance in attention. For the stronger power, its relationship with the weaker one forms only a small part of its total international interests, while for the weaker state this relationship may become overwhelmingly important to the point where it is likely to devote its attention with single-minded concentration to an uncomfortable situation and attempt to loosen or cut these ties. Thus, calculations based solely on economic power, that is on the ability to inflict punishment through economic means, are bound to be inadequate guides to the understanding of evolving relations.

International transactions may be said, in conclusion, to give rise to economic benefits which can be shared by the parties involved in these transactions. At the same time, however, international transactions may cause conflict over the distribution of these gains; and they can be used by one party to exploit the other politically and economically by deliberately manipulating conditions of dependence.

Economists typically take a different view of interdependence. They view interdependence as an unavoidable fact of life which is imposed on the shrinking world. National economies are becoming increasingly sensitive to their external environment and to actions taken by other economies. In the words of Professor Cooper, 'the central problem ... is how to keep the manifold benefits of extensive international economic intercourse free of crippling restrictions while at the same time preserving the maximum freedom for each nation to pursue its legitimate objectives'.[36]

Professor Cooper, then, sees interdependence as a constraint and is concerned with ways of limiting its negative effects. The view taken in this study is closer to that of Professor Hirschman and of the political scientists mentioned above.

We do not regard politics as external to economics. Instead, we view these two analytically separate spheres as mixed in reality; and it is the nature of that mixture that warrants further attention. Concepts and refinements of the notions of dependence and of interdependence are therefore discussed further in the following chapter.

Our ultimate purpose is to address the question of how to foster interdependence deliberately so that it will, indeed, act as a constraint – a constraint on the use of violence in international relations and as a factor which can stabilise peace between recent belligerents.

NOTES AND REFERENCES

1. See, for example, Edgar Feige, 'The Economic Consequences of Peace in the Middle East', *Challenge*, New York, January-February 1979; H. Askari and V. Corb, 'Economic Implications of Military Expenditures in the Middle East', *Journal of Peace Research*, Oslo, vol. XI, no. 4, 1974; and Henry J. Bruton, *The Promise of Peace: Economic Cooperation Between Egypt and Israel*, Staff Paper (Washington: Brookings Institution, 1980).

2. Kenneth E. Boulding, *The Economy of Love and Fear: a Preface to Grants Economics* (Belmont, California: Wadsworth, 1973).

3. John Maynard Keynes, *The Economic Consequences of the Peace*, reprinted edition (London:

Macmillan, 1971; and New York: St Martin's Press, 1971) p. xi (first edition printed in 1921).

4. See Anatol Rapoport, 'Prisoner's Dilemma: Recollections and Observations', in Rapoport (ed.), *Game Theory as a Theory of Conflict* (Dordrecht, Holland: Reidel, 1974).

5. Boulding, 'The Relations of Economic, Political and Social Systems', *Social and Economic Studies*, Mona, Jamaica, December 1962, pp. 351-62, republished in Boulding, *Towards a General Social Science, Collected Papers – Volume 4* (Boulder, Colorado: Colorado Associated University Press, 1974) pp. 148-62.

6. Johan Galtung's entry on 'Peace' in the *International Encyclopedia of the Social Sciences*, (London: Macmillan, 1968; and New York: the Free Press, 1968) vol. 11, p. 492.

7. Note for example the many years it takes for ex-colonies to change their trade relations with the former mother country.

8. Richard N. Cooper, 'Trade Policy is Foreign Policy', *Foreign Policy*, New York, Winter 1972-73.

9. Ideas presented by Edward L. Morse in his talk 'Interdependence: Promises and Pitfalls', at the International Conference on 'Towards Peace in the Middle East', Tel Aviv University, Tel Aviv, Israel, June 1979. For an intellectual history see Marcel Merle (ed.), *Pacifisme et Internationalisme* (Paris: Armand Colin, 1966); and Edmund Silberner (ed.), *La Guerre et la Paix dans l'Histoire des Doctrines Économiques* (Paris: Sirey, 1957).

10. Baron de Montesquieu, *De l'Esprit des Lois*, Book XX, ch. 2 in Oeuvres, vol. I (Amsterdam and Leipzig) p. 446, quoted in Albert O. Hirschman, *National Power and the Structure of Foreign Trade* (Berkeley: University of California Press, 1945) p. 10.

11. E. H. Carr, *The Twenty Years' Crisis, 1919-1939*, 2nd ed. (New York: Harper & Row, 1964) p. 53 (first edition published in 1939).

12. Carr, *op. cit.*, pp. 87-88. See also Kenneth N. Waltz, 'The Myth of National Interdependence', in Charles P. Kindleberger (ed.), *The International Corporation* (Cambridge, Mass.: MIT Press, 1970) pp. 205-23.

13. Hans J. Morgenthau, *Politics Among Nations: the Struggle for Power and Peace*, 5th ed. (New York: A.A. Knopf, 1973).

14. Morgenthau, 'The New Diplomacy of Movement', *Encounter*, London, August 1974.

15. Lester R. Brown, *World Without Borders* (New York: Random House, 1972).

16. Kindleberger, *American Business Abroad* (New Haven: Yale University Press, 1969) p. 207.

17. Robert O. Keohane and Joseph S. Nye, *Power and Interdependence* (Boston: Little, Brown, 1977) pp.3-4.

18. Carr, *The Future of Nations: Independence or Interdependence* (London: Kegan Paul, 1941).

19. *Ibid.*, p. 27.

20. Keohane and Nye, *op cit.*, p.4.

21. Raymond Vernon, *Sovereignty at Bay* (New York: Basic Books, 1971).

22. Keohane and Nye, *op. cit.*, pp. 11-18.

23. *Ibid.*

24. James A. Caporaso, 'Introduction', *International Organization*, Boston, Special issue, Winter 1978, pp. 1-12.

25. Caporaso, 'Dependence, Dependency, and Power in the Global System: a Structural and Behavioral Analysis', *International Organization*, Winter 1978, pp. 13-43.

26. Sanjaya Lall, 'Is "Dependence" a Useful Concept in Analyzing Underdevelopment', *World Development*, Oxford, vol. 3, nos. 11 and 12, 1975.

27. Caporaso, 'Dependence, Dependency, and Power in the Global System', *op. cit.*

28. See also Raymond D. Duvall, 'Dependence and Dependencia Theory: Notes Toward

Precision of Concept and Argument', *International Organization*, Winter 1978, pp. 51-78.

29. Th. Dos Santos, 'The Structure of Dependence', *American Economic Review*, Papers and Proceedings of the 82nd Annual Meeting of the American Economic Association, May 1970, p. 231.

30. Havelock R. Brewster, 'Economic Dependence: a Quantitative Interpretation', *Social and Economic Studies*, March 1973, p. 91.

31. Caporaso, 'Dependence, Dependency, and Power in the Global System', *op. cit.*

32. Fernando H. Cardoso, 'Associated Development', in A. Stepan (ed.), *Authoritarian Brazil: Policies and Futures* (New Haven: Yale University Press, 1973) p. 163.

33. Caporaso, 'Dependence, Dependency, and Power in the Global System', *op. cit.*

34. Hirschman, *op. cit.*, p. 16.

35. Hirschman, 'Beyond Asymmetry: Critical Notes on Myself as a Young Man and on Some Other Old Friends', *International Organization*, Winter 1978, pp. 45-50.

36. Cooper, *The Economics of Interdependence: Economic Policy in the Atlantic Community* (New York: McGraw-Hill, for the Council on Foreign Relations, 1968).

CHAPTER 2

Interdependence between Past Belligerents

When recent belligerents seek to develop bilateral relations, the point of departure is zero. Changes in the nature and extent of their relations are not at the margin; they are profound, since even a small volume of trade represents an infinite rate of change.

Government policies *vis-à-vis* the recent belligerent will inevitably be formulated within a specific context, taking into account the circumstances in which peace was achieved, the intensity of the conflict and the extent to which it was indeed resolved. Whatever the specifics of the situation, it can be assumed that, in formulating peace-time policies, each party seeks to avoid excessive dependence on the other.

Dependence, as was shown in Chapter 1, is not a state which can be easily defined or measured. All countries are affected by economic and other conditions in the rest of the world. In a sense, therefore, no country is completely independent. Absolute dependence, on the other hand, is also likely to be rare in the real world: some degree of dependence usually exists between any pair of countries. The degree of dependence can be increased or decreased by following conscious decisions made for political or economic reasons.

Since our concern is with the basis for establishing relationships which are not yet in existence, it is perhaps especially important to define and measure concepts such as dependence, that seemingly abstract term which, when applied to bilateral relationships, cannot be altogether avoided, and should not, under any circumstances, be too high.

DEPENDENCE

Following Professor Hirschman, we consider country A to be dependent on country B, provided that (i) A derives substantial benefits from its transactions with B and (ii) B is in the position to deprive A of these benefits. Both conditions must be satisfied if A is to be dependent on B.[1]

The meaning of 'dependence' in the present context may be clarified further by returning to the energy problem discussed in Chapter 1. Suppose A purchases from B all its petroleum, which is a major source of energy in A's economy. If petroleum were denied to A it would suffer substantial hardship, since petroleum plays a vital role in many economic activities and has few substitutes, at least in the short run, bearing in mind that switching to other sources of energy requires substantial investments and involves a long time lag. The fact that B supplies A with all or most of its petroleum does not in itself make A dependent on B. If A has access to alternative sources of supply at world market prices, it is not dependent on B. Dependence exists only if B has a monopoly over petroleum, or if for some reasons (which will be explored later) there is a substantial difference in the cost to A of obtaining petroleum from B and from alternative sources.

If A is dependent on B, B's ability to deprive A of economic welfare can be translated into what Professor Hirschman calls 'power relations'. B can use its economic power to force A into taking decisions it would not otherwise take. These decisions can be in the economic sphere (grant B's firms certain concessions or preferential treatment), the political sphere (join an alliance sponsored by B, support or oppose certain resolutions at the United Nations) or in the military sphere (change A's defence budget, change its military deployment and so on). A can avoid making the unpalatable decisions demanded by B only if it is willing to pay an economic price. Clearly, the larger the economic damage which B can inflict on A, the higher the price which it can exact in terms of political, economic or other concessions.

If A is dependent on B in the sense described above, the power which B wields over A at any point in time has been acquired as a result of A's past decisions regarding the level and composition of its economic transactions with B. A's present dependence on B could have been avoided or reduced had A at some crucial point in the past decided not to purchase certain essential materials from B, or to diversify its sources of supply.

The observation about the relationship between dependence at a given time and past decisions regarding intensity of bilateral economic transactions is particularly important in the context of peacemaking. Bilateral economic transactions between the recent belligerents at the time they make peace are likely to be non-existent. The decision on the volume and composition of economic transactions with B which A is willing to accept at the time economic relations are being initiated has important repercussions on its level of dependence on B in the future.

Let us examine the factors entering into the considerations of A as it seeks to determine the 'right' or 'optimal' level of bilateral economic transactions with its recent enemy and the manner in which these factors interact.

A first approximation of A's decision problem – that is, the determination of the level of bilateral transactions with B – is illustrated in Figure 2.1. The vertical axis shows the economic gains which A derives from transactions with B. The power B acquires over A through these transactions is shown on the horizontal axis and is labelled dependence. Both variables increase with the volume of transactions. An increase in transactions leads to higher economic

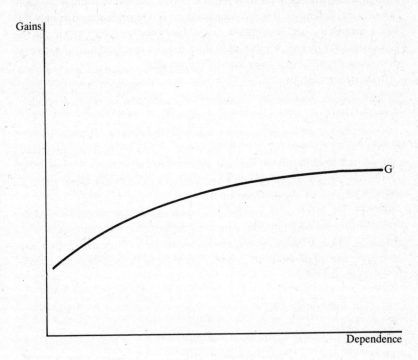

FIGURE 2.1
Economic Gains and Dependence

gains to A and to a greater dependence on B. A's greater dependence is reflected by its increasing reluctance to assert its independence as potential economic losses rise. The resulting relationship between economic gains and power (dependence) is depicted by the curve G in Figure 2.1. G rises with dependence, presumably at a declining rate. Like many other economic relationships, marginal benefits decline as total benefits increase, since the more profitable transactions presumably take precedence over the less profitable ones.

The sources of A's potential gains from its transactions with B, which were noted briefly in Chapter 1, are discussed in detail in Chapter 3. At this point, it is sufficient to note that these gains are made possible by savings in transfer costs which A must pay for transactions with alternative suppliers or buyers located further away than B. Additional gains may be derived from economies of scale. When A and B are neighbours, their combined markets may in some cases become large enough to enable certain industrial plants or other activities to reduce their unit costs to a level which enables them to compete internationally.[2] The level of gains thus represents the addition to A's national income derived from the difference between transacting with neighbouring B and with the more distant 'rest of the world' and, too, from the gains made possible by utilisation of economies of scale which the combined markets of A and B make possible.

A must decide on the appropriate trade-offs between economic gains, on the one side, and dependence, on the other. A must choose the preferred point on the feasible set G. At that point, marginal economic gains from additional transactions with B will be just offset by A's dislike of yet another incremental unit of dependence on B.

The people involved in making that kind of decision would surely feel more comfortable about it if the notion of 'dependence' were represented by something more tangible, more easily measurable. They might find the concept of 'cost of dissociation', which is introduced in the following section, to be quite helpful.

COST OF DISSOCIATION

Cost of dissociation, as the phrase implies, is that cost which A incurs if B decides to sever economic relations with it. A's gains from bilateral transactions with B materialise only if these transactions take place. The decision to transact, however, depends on both A and B. Assuming that A wishes to engage in bilateral transactions with B, then it is up to the latter to decide whether to transact with A and whether the level of transactions desired by A is acceptable. If A's economy is geared to a certain level of transactions with B, then A becomes dependent on B, in the sense that B can inflict economic hardship on A by unilaterally discontinuing these transactions or by 'dissociating'. Costs of dissociation obviously rise with the level of gains which A derives from its transactions with B. A's readiness to assume the risk of having to incur these costs will depend, to an important degree, on their level. Since the costs of dissociation are measurable, they can serve as a proxy for the more problematic concept of 'dependence'.

Costs of dissociation are strictly defined as the change in national income following dissociation. Thus, if B discontinues economic transactions with neighbouring A, A incurs costs of dissociation borne by both its producers and consumers.[3]

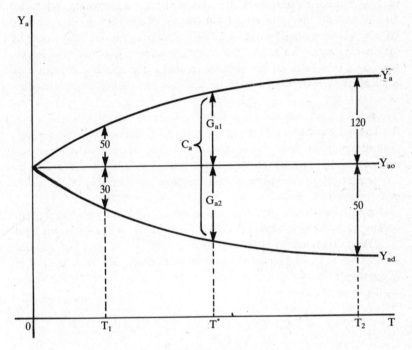

FIGURE 2.2
A's National Product under Different Conditions

Costs of dissociation are nearly always higher than the gains from bilateral transactions. To see why this is so, consider a typical trade transaction which peace between A and B makes possible. Let us assume that a specific transaction is found to be profitable and that in order to export to B, A has to increase production capacity. For this purpose, resources must be diverted from other uses. Capital must be mobilised and invested in plant and equipment, labour must be hired away from alternative employment and trained to perform new functions, stocks of raw material must be expanded and so on. Some of these resources represent a permanent investment. They cannot be recovered if the planned transactions fail to materialise after the investment takes place. Some of the equipment has no alternative uses. If labour is specialised it has to be retrained before it can be used elsewhere. Stocks of raw materials and of finished products may be too large for the reduced level of activity following the closure of the export market. It must thus be concluded that if dissociation takes place, some economic resources are permanently lost. This means that the cost of dissociation borne by A is greater than the gains it enjoys from bilateral transactions with B. A's costs of dissociation equal the gains from these transactions plus the loss in A's national income due to its inability to utilise the specialised factors of production permanently invested in activities generating bilateral transactions with B.

Figure 2.2 illustrates the relationship between A's national income (Y_a), A's cost of dissociation (C_a) and the gains from transactions (G_{a1}), given different levels of these transactions (T). Y_{ao} is the level of A's national income if A and B do not transact; that is, when $T = O$. Y_a rises as T rises. If, for example, the amount of transactions reaches T_1, then $Y_a(T_1) = Y_{ao} + 5O$, or if transactions reach T_2, then $Y_a(T_2) = Y_{ao} + 12O$.

If dissociation occurs, A's national income, Y_a, does not revert to Y_{ao} but declines to Y_{ad}, which is lower than Y_{ao}: for example, to $Y_{ao} - 3O$ if the level of planned transactions is T_1, or to $Y_{ao} - 5O$ if the level of planned transactions is T_2. The higher the level of transactions, the larger the loss of A's national income, G_{a2}, in case of dissociation. Thus, A's costs of dissociation, C_a, are:

$$C_a = G_{a1} + G_{a2} = Y_a - Y_{ad}$$

and

$$G_{a2} = Y_{ao} - Y_{ad}$$

INTERDEPENDENCE

The definition of dependence proposed in the last section is based on the notion that A is dependent on B if the latter can deny the former welfare gains made possible by bilateral transactions between them. The denial of these gains leads to costs of dissociation which A may be reluctant to bear. When such costs are unacceptable, A is said to be dependent on B.

The fact that A imports certain goods from B does not in itself make A dependent on B. Since both countries gain from bilateral exchange, A is not only dependent on B; B is also dependent on A. Under these circumstances, relative rather than absolute dependence will determine the power relations between the two parties. Relative dependence can be determined only once it is known which of the two parties gains more from the transaction. The exporter is, in principle, just as dependent on the markets as the importer is on suppliers. In either case, dissociation can cause substantial hardships. The case of oil mentioned earlier, rather than constituting an exception, actually confirms this thesis. Saudi Arabia grows very little food, while most of her clients have access to some alternative sources of energy. Hence, Saudi Arabia is more dependent on imports for her economic well being than most of her clients are dependent on her for oil. The same applies to OPEC members and their clients as a group. OPEC's strength derives from the ability of its members to organise a fairly disciplined cartel. If the oil consumers could muster the political will and the discipline to negotiate as a single entity, rather than bid against each other for OPEC's restricted supplies, they could, without doubt, reduce substantially the real price of oil.

Countries which trade intensively – that is, where a high proportion of their consumption consists of imports – are by definition trade dependent. This, however, does not mean that they are dependent in the sense discussed above. Dependence on international trade does not necessarily expose a country to high costs of dissociation. These can be minimised by both product and market diversification. Trade dependence becomes dependence in the present sense only if a high proportion of total trade is bilateral and if shifting to other suppliers or markets turns out to be very costly. In this case, trade dependence could lead to high costs of dissociation, if substantial resources employed in facilitating these transactions have no alternative employment. Even if A finds itself in a situation where the costs of dissociating from B are indeed high, A's vulnerability could be reduced if B's costs of dissociation were also high.

One-way dependence, therefore, is not the only possible outcome of economic relations between two countries. Bilateral transactions can lead to mutual dependence or interdependence. Two countries are said to be interdependent when the cost of dissociation of both, regardless of who decides to dissociate, is balanced in the sense that dissociation for one country is more or less as painful as it is for the other.

The concept of interdependence and the relationship between dependence and interdependence are illustrated graphically in Figure 2.3.

A's costs of dissociation (C_a) are shown on the horizontal axis and B's (C_b)

on the vertical axis. Looked at from A's point of view, movement along the horizontal axis denotes increasing dependence on B, since A's costs of dissociation increase while B's remain constant. A vertical move, by contrast,

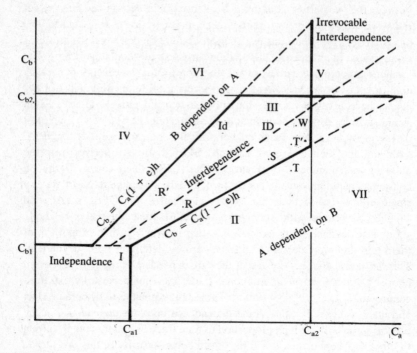

FIGURE 2.3
Determination of Independence, Dependence and Interdependence

denotes an increase in B's dependence on A. Interdependence is represented as a first approximation by a ray through the origin, ID. ID denotes all the points where the costs of dissociation to B, C_b, are proportional to those to A, C_a.

$$ID = \{ (C_a, C_b); \ C_b = hC_a \}$$

in which h is a positive constant which is used to 'correct' the ratio of dissociation costs so as to accord with A's or B's notion of interdependence. It varies with both countries' economic size as represented by national income or a similar economic indicator. If both countries were of roughly equal size, h would presumably be equal to unity. To regard itself as interdependent with B, country A would probably insist on equality of dissociation costs with the former. If, however, the two economies are not equal, the smaller country is likely to insist on higher absolute costs being incurred by the larger one before regarding itself as being interdependent with it. Thus h is established by each country in accordance with its preferences, experience and expectations regarding the behaviour of the other party.

The straight line depicted by ID divides the area of Figure 2.3 into two basic regions: the region lying to the north-west of the line denotes B's dependence on A and the area lying to the south-east of the line denotes A's dependence on B. As a first approximation, interdependence is represented by ID, the line separating the two areas. This interpretation of interdependence appears too narrow, since obviously both sides will accept some deviation from ID before they regard themselves as being dependent on the other. The permitted deviation, e, is assumed to increase with the absolute value of C_a and C_b.

Again, using formal notation, interdependence, like dependence, is represented by a region Id which has the following characteristics:

$$Id = \{ (C_a, C_b); \ h(1 - e) < C_b/C_a < h(1 + e) \}$$

Id is a region where the ratio of dissociation costs varies within an acceptable range (e) from a predetermined ratio (h). Specifically, Id is the area between the lines where:

$$C_b = hC_a(1 + e)$$

and

$$C_b = hC_a(1 - e)$$

B is dependent on A if $C_b > C_a(1 + e)h$
   (region IV in Figure 2.3);
A is dependent on B if $C_b < C_a(1 - e)h$
   (region II in Figure 2.3);
A and B are interdependent if $C_a(1 - e)h < C_b < C_a(1 + e)h$
   (region III in Figure 2.3).

To complete the picture and make it more realistic, we introduce four more regions labelled independence (region I in Figure 2.3), irrevocable dependence (regions VI and VII) and irrevocable interdependence (region V in Figure 2.3). The delineation of these regions is facilitated by the introduction of minimum and maximum threshold costs of dissociation: C_{a1}, C_{a2}, C_{b1} and C_{b2}, respectively. As long as C_a is less than C_{a1}, A considers itself as being independent of B, even if B's dissociation costs are less than indicated by the required ratio. The other extreme is reached when C_a

TABLE 2.1

Determination of Independence, Dependence and Interdependence
(Symbolic Presentation)

	$C_a \leqslant C_{a1}$	$C_{a1} < C_a < C_{a2}$	$C_a \geqslant C_{a2}$
$C_b \leqslant C_{b1}$	Independence	A dependent on B	A dependent on B
$C_{b1} < C_b < C_{b2}$ and $h(1 - e) < C_b/C_a < h(1 + e)$	B dependent on A	Interdependence	A dependent on B
$C_{b1} < C_b < C_{b2}$ and $C_b/C_a \leqslant h(1 - e)$	B dependent on A	A dependent on B	A dependent on B
$C_{b1} < C_b < C_{b2}$ and $C_b/C_a \geqslant h(1 + e)$	B dependent on A	B dependent on A	A dependent on B
$C_b \geqslant C_{b2}$	B dependent on A	B dependent on A	Irrevocable interdependence

exceeds C_{a2}, the maximum threshold. In that case, A regards itself as being irrevocably dependent on B, unless B's dissociation costs exceed its own maximum threshold, C_{b2}, in which case both are irrevocably interdependent. Irrevocability in the present context implies that the costs of dissociation are not acceptable to the country which must incur these costs. Supplementing Figure 2.3, Table 2.1 lists all possible relations between A and B and the conditions which must be fulfilled if these relations are to hold.

The distinction between regions of independence, dependence, interdependence and irrevocable interdependence makes it possible to focus on the relationship between these 'states' and on the policies which A and B can follow to achieve the relationships they like and to avoid those which they reject.

A is independent of B as long as costs of dissociation are less than a specified minimum, C_{a1}. If A wants to avoid dependence, it will presumably not accept an increase in bilateral transactions with B, beyond C_{a1}, even if it increases its economic welfare, unless mutual dependence or interdependence is at an acceptable level. Thus A may accept a move from R to S but not from R to T even if T yields more economic gains than S.

Additional insights may be gained by considering the transition from ordinary to irrevocable interdependence. Interdependence becomes irrevocable when the costs of dissociation are too high to be acceptable. When the costs of dissociation become so large as seriously to disrupt the economic well being of the parties in question, dissociation becomes unthinkable. If A and B could be induced to move to the region of irrevocable interdependence, peace between them would be more secure.

Figure 2.3 illustrates some of the pitfalls which must be guarded against on the way. The shaded areas which appear on the border of region V are of particular significance in this case. They indicate that the transition from interdependence to irrevocable interdependence is not necessarily smooth, involving simply the acceptance.of more bilateral transactions by both A and B. Successful accomplishment of the transition may require a quantum jump which, if not sufficiently large, may lead to an intolerable level of dependence by A on B or *vice versa*. As A approaches C_{a2} and B, C_{b2}, they may well become more, rather than less, cautious as they consider further expansion of their economic relations. Added caution may take the form of insistence on formal agreements or institutional devices which help to reduce the possibility of dissociation by the other side.

Figure 2.3 also illustrates the potential conflict or lack of harmony between the 'public' and the 'private' interest. There is no market mechanism which guarantees that transactions considered by individual firms in A or B will leave the two countries within the required bounds. While most transactions voluntarily agreed upon benefit both sides, which implies a move in the north-east direction, a move from point R to T, which is the 'right' direction, nevertheless results in A stepping over the boundary of interdependence and becoming dependent on B. The public view of a transaction depends also on the cumulative effect of all the other transactions that take place. Consequently, potential conflict between the private and the public interest threatens to affect any transaction contemplated by individual actors. Under these circumstances it is extremely difficult to formulate policies or guidelines for dealing with the past enemy, since individual transactions which in one case may be perfectly consistent with the public interest may be considered as harmful at a different point in time, even when the policy itself remains unchanged. Thus a transaction moving the parties from R to T will, presumably, be vetoed by those responsible for public policy making in A. An identical transaction (identical in terms of economic benefits and changes in the level of dissociation costs) which will move the parties from R' to T' will be entirely welcome. This example illustrates the importance of establishing the right kind of institutional mechanisms in the course of stabilising peace between recent belligerents. The example also demonstrates the necessity of supervising private transactions in the name of the public interest and the great difficulty of devising long-term guidelines which will replace detailed intervention by public authorities. These issues will be taken up in greater detail in the following chapter.

INTERDEPENDENCE AND DETERRENCE

The approach used here to describe the relationship between costs of dissociation and interdependence can be extended to encompass the concept of deterrence or balance of terror, which was discussed in Chapter 1. Both approaches represent attempts by A and B to avoid unacceptable domination by the other by different means. Balance of terror is achieved through negative interdependence. Positive interdependence, achieved through economic transactions while avoiding imbalance in costs of dissociation, can bring about the same results.

A graphic presentation of deterrence can be obtained by extending Figure 2.3 in the south-west direction, as is shown in Figure 2.4. The addition to the vertical axis is now labelled destructive capacity of B (D_b) and the extension of the horizontal axis is labelled destructive capacity of A, (D_a). These capacities are acquired through expenditures on arms and other military means. They represent, of course, the diversion of real resources from alternative income-enhancing uses.

Each country seeks to deter the other against aggression by maintaining a level of destructive capacity such that D_a/D_b does not exceed the ratio m by more than e, an acceptable deviation. If, for example, A increases its destructive capacity such that

$$D_a > D_b(m + e)$$

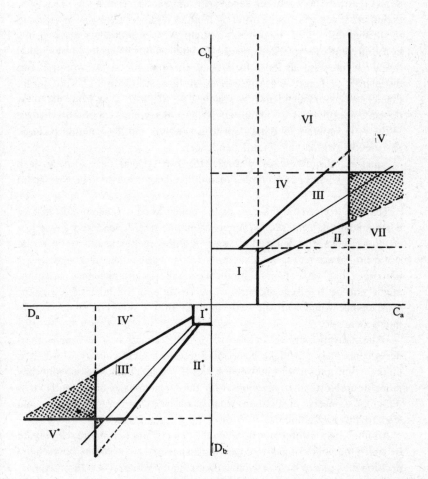

FIGURE 2.4
Interdependence and Deterrence

then B will increase its own capacity in order to counterbalance the threat posed by A and bring the ratio of destructive capacities back into line. If B fails to increase its defence outlays, it becomes subject to military blackmail by A. As shown in Figure 2.4, it is possible to distinguish between different regions which are analogous to those outlined in Figure 2.3 and which also depict the transition between superiority and equivalence. As in Figure 2.3, the different regions denote different degrees of power relations. Whereas in the former case interdependence is brought about by mutual economic gains, in the present case interdependence, or equivalence, is achieved by mutual threat, giving rise in turn to mutual economic loss. Accordingly, we distinguish in Figure 2.4 between the following regions: I^* – no threat (analogous to independence in Figure 2.3); II^* – B is superior to A (A dependent on B); III^* – mutual equivalence-deterrence (interdependence); IV^* – A is superior to B (B dependent on A); and V^* – mutual assured destruction (irrevocable interdependence).[4]

Some of the differences between the two systems have already been discussed in Chapter 1. A number of additional points ought to be considered here.

The first concerns the nature of the policy when it is successful; that is, when stability is achieved. Whereas economic interdependence yields real economic gains, the deterrence system requires real expenditures to create sufficient capacity to cause unacceptable damage to the other side. Note, however, that some regions in the economic interdependence situations might not be feasible. In such cases no amount of bilateral economic transactions would lead the two countries into a situation of irrevocable interdependence.

Alternatively, and this is the more likely situation, irrevocable interdependence may not make economic sense in a multi-country world. It is unlikely that transactions between A and B will in all cases be economically more desirable than transactions with third countries. Consequently, it is difficult to conceive of situations where economic considerations alone could lead to the realisation of irrevocable interdependence.[5]

Another major difference between the two systems pertains to the method by which the policy objective could be reached and the confidence which the decision makers can have in leading their country into irrevocable situations.

Under the deterrence system, each country makes its own decisions, possibly after reaching agreements with the other side, but not knowing exactly how its counterpart will behave. Under positive interdependence, decisions are made simultaneously by the two parties with the full knowledge and agreement of both. Non-cooperation, which can lead to any position in the deterrence system, leads only to independence in the positive interdependence system. In this case, each side is aware of the actions of the other and bases its decisions on its estimate of its own costs of dissociation and on those of the other country.

The deterrence system, on the other hand, allows each party to take unilateral decisions regarding the level of destructive capacity which it intends to acquire. Each party's decisions are based on its own objectives and available resources, on the one hand, and on the resources, perceived objectives and the known or estimated destructive capacity of the other party, on the other hand. As one party executes its policy the other amends its own decisions so as to adjust to the new situation. Under such circumstances it is necessary to formulate a strategy which takes into account the built-in uncertainty concerning the moves of the other party and which may well lead to instability.

The situation confronting the parties and the process of decision making is most aptly represented by two-person non-zero-sum games where one party's losses can be higher or lower than the other party's gains, and where the decisions are based on both incomplete and uncertain information and the outcomes depend on what the two sides will do. Situations approximated by two-person non-zero-sum games are inherently complex and unstable.

Positive interdependence, of the kind depicted in Figure 2.3 and the north-east portion of Figure 2.4, can be handled within the framework of less complex methods leading to stable solutions. This is due to the fact that each transaction must by definition be agreed upon in advance by both parties; thus, most elements of uncertainty inherent in the deterrence system are missing. Since the level of transactions is mutually determined, it is possible to calculate the costs of dissociation of both parties with a relatively high degree of confidence.

Accordingly, the decision-making process will tend to focus on the selection of an optimal level of economic transactions, taking into account the potential economic gains if transactions materialise, the potential costs of dissociation and the probabilities of both events. The methodology used to handle this type of decision problem will, therefore, be different from the methodology used in the deterrence system. The nature of the solutions is also different: instability and suspicion prevail in the deterrence situation versus equilibrium (stability) and relative mutual confidence when both parties manage to agree on choosing the route of interdependence.

MAXIMISING EXPECTED GAINS

By introducing the concept of costs of dissociation we have made a step in the direction of quantifying A's decision problem. A's problem can be viewed as choosing a level of bilateral transactions which will represent an acceptable trade-off between gains from these transactions if they materialise and the cost of dissociation which it will incur if the planned transactions fail to materialise. The link between these two events, so far missing, is the probability associated with dissociation. If ˌthe probability of dissociation, given different levels of transactions, were known, or could be estimated with reasonable confidence, the decision problem would be much simplified. Dissociation can occur either through intentional disruption by one of the parties or due to some accidental cause which should be taken into account. The probability of dissociation is the probability, as seen by A, of B's dissociating after transactions have been agreed upon.

TABLE 2.2
Economic Gains, Costs of Dissociation and Expected Income
(an Example)

Trans-actions level	G_{a1}	Y_a	G_{a2}	Y_{ad}	P_a	$1 - P_a$	Expected national income
T_1	50	$Y_{oa} + 50$	30	$Y_{oa} - 30$	0.8	0.2	$34 + Y_{oa}$
T_2	120	$Y_{oa} + 120$	50	$Y_{oa} - 50$	0.5	0.5	$35 + Y_{oa}$

The level and distribution of the probability of dissociation reflects in some sense B's benevolence towards A or, more precisely, A's view of B's attitude towards it and of B's stability in general. If the probability distribution is known, it is possible to calculate the expected national income of A for each level of transactions. Table 2.2 contains examples of such computations. Expected gains associated with two levels of bilateral transactions are computed. If transactions reach T_1 (shown in Figure 2.3), A's gains will be $50 million. If the transaction fails to materialise, A's national income will be lower by $80 million. There is an 80 per cent chance, according to A's evaluations, that B will transact at the level of T_1. This implies a 20 per cent chance of dissociation. Expected national income, E_t, is calculated as follows:

$$E_t = P_t Y_t + (1 - P_t)Y_{td} = Y_{to} + P_t G_{t1} - (1 - P_t)G_{t2}$$

where

t	=	country index (t = a,b)
P_t	=	the probability that the other country will decide to transact
$1 - P_t$	=	the probability that the other country will decide to dissociate
Y_{to}	=	national income if bilateral transactions are not contemplated
Y_t	=	national income if bilateral transactions take place
Y_{td}	=	national income if dissociation occurs after resources are committed to bilateral transactions
G_t	=	gains from bilateral transactions

Using the figures pertaining to T_1 in Table 2.2, expected national income can be calculated:

$$E_a = (Y_{oa} + 50)0.8 + (Y_{oa} - 30)0.2 = 34 + Y_{oa}$$

Table 2.2 contains a second example pertaining to a higher transactions level – T_2. In this case, gains and costs of dissociation are higher – $80 million and $170 million respectively. The probability of transaction taking place is also different – it is assumed to have declined to 50 per cent, which raises the probability of dissociation to 50 per cent. Expected gains in this case are $35 million. Similar computations can be made for any level of transactions. If the information about the gains from bilateral transactions, the costs of dissociation and the probability of dissociation attached to the different levels of bilateral transactions were available, an appropriate decision rule for A would be to maximise expected gains from bilateral transactions or, equivalently, to maximise expected national income. This familiar rule is applicable to many situations in which the decision maker is risk neutral and can estimate the gains he will make if the venture he is considering is successful, the loss he will incur if the venture fails and the odds of each possible outcome.

RISK OF DISSOCIATION

The analysis in the last section of the decision problem which A faces – namely, establishing an optimal level of transactions with B – led to the conclusion that the relevant factors entering A's decision are the value of gains, the costs of dissociation and the probability of dissociation attached to different levels of transactions.

It is this last point which is most troublesome when one tries to apply perfectly reasonable decision rules to 'real life' situations. Information about the probability of dissociation is of crucial importance in the present context. Transactions level T_2 is preferred to T_1 if B decides to transact with A. T_1 is preferred if B decides to dissociate. Moreover, if B decides to dissociate, a zero level of transactions is better still. Thus far it has been assumed that the probability of B's decision to dissociate is somehow determined exogenously; that is, by B's benevolence towards A and other considerations which are independent of the level, composition and profitability of the bilateral transactions between the two parties. This assumption is now re-examined and modified.

Since nearly all bilateral transactions give rise to dissociation costs for both countries, this should clearly affect the probability of B's (and A's) decision to dissociate. In general, one can expect this probability to be negatively correlated with the costs of dissociation.

The inclusion of the other party's dissociation costs, among the factors which A must consider when it seeks to establish an appropriate level of bilateral transactions with B, affects the decision-making rule. A no longer operates in a world in which it decides unilaterally on how to trade uncertain gains against uncertain losses. A can affect the uncertainty which it faces, changing the level and distribution of the probability of dissociation, thus transforming it from an exogenous into an endogenous decision variable.

The probability of dissociation, as seen by A, can be changed by influencing B's costs of dissociation. Other things being equal, B's propensity to dissociate is a declining function of these costs. By the same token, B's propensity to dissociate is a declining function of its own gains from bilateral transactions.

Economic gains from bilateral transactions between A and B can be assumed, as we have argued, to increase with the volume of bilateral transactions (T) and are shared by both parties. We denote total mutual gains from transactions of volume T by $z(T)$ and A's share by k. In this case A's gains are $kz(T)$ and B's gains are $(1-k)z(T)$. The ratio $k/(1-k)$ represents the relative gains from bilateral transactions. The larger is k, the higher is A's share of total gains and the lower B's share. Here k is akin to the concept of terms of trade, familiar from international trade theory. A can affect B's propensity to dissociate by accepting a smaller share of total gains $z(T)$.

The gain of each country from bilateral transactions, $G_{tl}(T)$ $(t = a,b)$, is not necessarily limited to its share of total gains $z(T)$. It can be increased by unilateral commitment of resources to activities facilitating such transactions: establishing sales offices in the other country, investing in infra-structure projects, adapting products to the specifications of the other country and so on.

It is because of these investments, denoted here by I_t ($t = a,b$), that costs of dissociation are always higher than the gains from bilateral transactions. The level of long-range commitments required to facilitate transactions of a given volume is not necessarily fixed; there is probably a range of possible substitution between fixed investments and variable costs. For example, over a given range of output it is usually possible to substitute capital for labour. This leads to a reduction in total unit costs, provided a higher volume of sales materialises.

The decision on the level of fixed investments is obviously influenced by the riskiness of the investment. Often a lower level of investment will be preferred, even though it yields a lower expected profit rate, because it is also less risky. On the other hand, the two sides can reassure each other about their long-range intentions by following the above strategy. This way, both increase their gains from bilateral transactions and increase their losses from dissociation. Thus, if A increases its long-range investments in bilateral transactions with B, this serves as notice to B that it does not intend to dissociate.

We assume here that the additional gains from fixed investments (I_t) accrue only to country t where the investments originate. Thus we write:

$IG_t(I_t,T)$ = gains accruing to t ($t = a,b$) from investments I_t relating to bilateral transactions of volume T

IG_1 is assumed to increase with both I_t and T.

$$G_{a1}(I_a,T) = kz(T) + IG_a(I_a,T) = Y_a - Y_{ao}$$

$$G_{b1}(I_b,T) = (1 - k)z(T) + IG_b(I_b,T) = Y_b - Y_{bo}$$

$$G_{t2}(I_t,T) = Y_{to} - Y_{td} \qquad t = (a,b)$$

where, as before

G_{t1} = total gains of country t from bilateral transactions if transactions materialise

G_{t2} = the loss of each country from dissociation after resources are committed to bilateral transactions. G_{t2} increases with both the level of transactions T and the level of investments I_t

The costs of dissociation, C_t, are:

$$C_t = Y_t - Y_{td} = G_{t1} + G_{t2} \qquad (t = a,b)$$

Finally, let us re-examine P_t, the probability of transactions materialising. From A's point of view, P_a is a function of B's dissociation costs. The larger are B's losses from dissociation, the larger the probability that it will decide to refrain from dissociating. Thus we write:

$$P_a(C_b) = \text{the probability that B will transact,}$$

$$P_a{}'(C_b) > 0;$$

$$P_b(C_a) = \text{the probability that A will transact,}$$

$$P_b{}'(C_a) > 0$$

Each country is thus faced with the problem of maximising its expected national income. Each country selects an optimal level of bilateral transactions, T, given the initial terms of trade. It is not sufficient, however, for each country to decide on its optimal level of transactions. If transactions are to materialise, these two levels must coincide. The convergence of the two different levels of required transactions to a common one is reached through adjustments in the relative shares of gains from bilateral transactions between the parties.

Denoting the desired level of transactions by an asterisk, consider a case where $T_a{}^* > T_b{}^*$: A desires a higher level of transactions than B. A can offer several courses of action which might induce B to accept a higher level of transactions. A can offer B a higher share in the gains. This can be done by changing k or by altering the price of inputs or outputs of some or all transactions.[6] The change in k will in turn increase B's cost of dissociation (C_b) and the probability that B will decide to transact (P_a). P_b can also be influenced, as shown above, by increasing A's investments in bilateral transactions, which increases A's costs of dissociation, thus reassuring B about A's intentions towards future bilateral transactions.

The formal presentation of the equilibrium conditions, that is, those where the terms of trade for which the optimal level of transactions chosen by the two countries coincide, is presented in Appendix 1. The analysis shows that the problem can be solved analytically. For both A and B there exists a common level of transactions, T, and investment levels, I_t ($t = a,b$), such that the expected value of bilateral transactions is maximised.

Several observations which are not intuitively obvious are suggested by the mathematical analysis. They concern the point of optimum; that is, the level of transactions and investments which maximise expected national income. At this point:

(1) Expected marginal gains at the optimal level of transactions (T) are positive.[7] This means that additional transactions could yield additional gains. The countries are willing to forego these additional gains because of the increase in the probability of dissociation associated with a higher level of costs of dissociation.

(2) Expected marginal gains from transacting are equal to marginal probable losses from dissociation.[8]

(3) The odds of dissociation equal the ratio of marginal gains to marginal losses from investments.[9]

Both the second and third conditions are reminiscent of the familiar profit maximisation rules: equalise marginal revenues to marginal costs. In the present case, however, the conditions are somewhat more complex because we are dealing with an uncertain world in which both gains from transactions and investments and the probability of receiving those gains are determined by the level of transactions.

To summarise, a number of methods can be used to affect the propensity of A and B to engage in bilateral transactions. These are (i) change the level of bilateral transactions, (ii) change the terms of trade and (iii) change the level of investments in bilateral transactions. Each one of these factors will affect the cost and probability of dissociation.

The system contains sufficient degrees of freedom to allow the two parties to arrive at an equilibrium – that is, a mutually acceptable level of bilateral transactions. The parties, in other words, possess a sufficient variety of policy instruments to arrive at a mutually acceptable level of transactions which allows both to reach a satisfactory trade-off between economic gains, on the one hand, and an increase in dependence, on the other.

INTERDEPENDENCE: A DYNAMIC PERSPECTIVE

The previous section examined the problem of establishing the 'right' level of bilateral transactions between recent belligerents within a static framework. It was implicitly assumed that an equilibrium can be achieved instantaneously and, more important, that once achieved it will be maintained automatically. Dynamic elements thus far have not been explicitly considered, although the time element was partly taken into account when analysing investments which A and B make to increase the profitability of bilateral transactions and which serve, incidentally, to decrease the probability of dissociation because of their positive impact on dissociation costs. It was shown earlier that if investments could be liquidated instantaneously at prices reflecting their full costs, costs of dissociation would be equal to the gains from bilateral transactions. It is the likelihood of substantial losses being incurred due to the inability to realise the full value of some investments made to promote bilateral transactions which gives rise to the discrepancy between gains from bilateral transactions and losses from dissociation.

This point can be clarified further by considering once again the energy problem already discussed at the beginning of this chapter. The disruptive effect of the oil-price rise would have been much smaller had it not been for the huge investments in oil-dependent activities, which have no alternative use, or which can be converted into alternative uses only at very high costs. Thus the world is dependent on oil not only because oil is (or rather was) so much cheaper than, say, coal. It is also – perhaps primarily – dependent on oil because of the long time lag and enormous resources which must be invested in conversion from oil to alternative fuels. The cost of dissociating from oil thus includes the outlay on complementary investments in power-generating capacity and in other energy-using installations.

This example and the preceding discussion illustrate the two important respects in which the value of investments and, hence, the value of both gains from bilateral transactions and costs of dissociation are affected by the time factor: the length of time during which they have no alternative use and the timing of new investment decisions. Both factors ought to be explicitly introduced into the decision-making process involving the determination of an optimal level of bilateral transactions.

Difficulties may also arise due to changes in the value of gains or costs associated with transactions based on projects having a long life. The following example, which illustrates this point, is based on a project which has been mentioned as a possible harbinger of Egyptian-Israeli economic cooperation.

Israel, as is well known, is relatively short of water. Her annual supply, which is less than 2,000 million cubic metres, is very unevenly distributed between the relatively rain-abundant north and the arid south.

Egypt gets most of her water supply from the Nile, which has an annual yield of about 85,000 million cubic metres. Of this amount, Egypt gets about 55,000 million and Sudan 30,000 million cubic metres. Since water-short Israel is a reputable exporter of professional services associated with irrigation and agriculture, she could offer Egypt the following arrangement: Israeli water and agricultural experts would undertake to increase the effective yield of the Nile to Egypt by, say, 5 per cent or about 2,000 million cubic metres. This could be done by improvements in drainage, irrigation, crop choice, crop rotation or a combination of these methods. Of the additional 2,000 million cubic metres thus made available, Egypt would undertake to sell one-quarter or 500 million cubic metres to Israel. If the arrangement is technically feasible, Egypt will gain 1,500 million and Israel 500 million cubic metres on a permanent basis.

The economics and engineering of such a project have yet to be studied in detail. Assume, however, that the investments required to raise the yield of the Nile and to bring the water across the Sinai can be shown to yield acceptable returns to both parties; and consider its implications for interdependence.

These can be quite disturbing, even if the benefits of such a scheme are fairly and equitably distributed and even if they are perpetual. Time in this case is likely to affect differently the value of the projects as seen by Egypt and Israel. Egypt at the project's inception enjoys benefits in the form of technological improvements which yield permanent gains represented by the value of 2,000 million cubic metres of water per annum. Part of this additional water she commits herself to selling to Israel in full or partial payment for the benefits she receives. This payment (500 million cubic metres of water per annum) is in time seen as a net reduction in resources available to Egypt.

Israel in turn makes investments at time zero for which she is supposed to be paid in perpetuity. The added water, which constitutes, under our assumption, 25 per cent of Israel's total supply in 1980, can make a potentially important contribution to the agricultural and industrial development of the Negev, Israel's arid south.

If ten or twenty years later Israel were to be deprived of the water imported from Egypt, she would face considerable hardship. Egypt is thus handed a leverage which she might be sorely tempted to use if only to raise the price of water she charges Israel.

Here, then, is an example of a situation where balanced interdependence at time zero can be transformed into one-way dependence some time later, simply because the benefits which the sides derive from the same transaction change disproportionately over time. Situations such as these can be foreseen. They can be taken care of by making sure that the balance of benefits accruing to both parties does not get too badly out of line at any foreseeable point in time.

NOTES AND REFERENCES

1. See Hirschman, *National Power and the Structure of Foreign Trade, op. cit.*

2. For a detailed analysis of these cases see Chapter 3.

3. The exact nature of these costs is explored in some detail in Chapter 3.

4. Mutual assured destruction is said to exist between two powers when '... neither can strike first at the other without receiving a completely intolerable retaliatory blow in return'. See Glenn H. Snyder, *Deterrence and Defence* (Princeton, N.J.: Princeton University Press, 1961) p. 41.

5. It could perhaps be argued that states consist of regions characterised by irrevocable interdependence. Such a proposition is reminiscent of the Optimum Currency Area, argued by Ronald I. McKinnon, of Stanford University. It is, however, far from self-evident.

6. The mechanisms for changing k are not easy to establish because of two complicating factors: (i) the exchange rates of A's and B's currencies are not determined solely by their bilateral transactions (they are also determined by their respective transactions with the rest of the world) and (ii) transactions are discrete, each transaction involving different actors.

7. From equation (A.1) we get:

$$E[dG_t/dT] = P_t \; dG_{t1}/dT + (1 - P_t) \; dG_t/dT > 0 \qquad (t = a,b).$$

8. From equation (A.1) we get:

$$C_t \; dPt/dT = E[dG_t/dT] \qquad (t = a,b).$$

9. From equation (A.2) we get:

$$(1 - P_t)/P_t = dIG_t/dI_t \; / \; dG_{t2}/dI_t \qquad (t = a,b).$$

CHAPTER 3

Peacemaking, Vested Interests and International Transactions

Chapter 2 considered the determination of the level of bilateral transactions and their overall impact on interdependence. The focus in this chapter shifts to the internal effects of such transactions, their effects on economic welfare and its distribution and their effect on the attitude to peace or to what is termed here the vested interest in peace.

It is easy to show that if economic relations between past belligerents are allowed to develop and activities such as trade in goods, trade in services, investments and joint ventures take place, economic welfare in both countries can increase. International economic transactions, while potentially beneficial to all parties, also tend to give rise to conflicts over the distribution of costs and gains within the two countries. These conflicts could easily have internal political repercussions. For the foreseeable future, specific economic transactions are likely to be evaluated by the governments of A and B, the recent belligerents, not only (and not even primarily) on the basis of their economic merits but also on their expected impact on the acceptance of peace by the public.

VESTED INTEREST IN PEACE

The analysis which follows starts from the premise that each of the two governments seeks to promote vested interest in peace. *Ceteris paribus*, each government can be thought of as seeking to maximise vested interest in peace. We assume that economic welfare and political views are related through a simple causal chain. Political support for a policy increases if it can be demonstrated that economic welfare will improve as a result of the policy's implementation. If this view of the formation of political opinions corresponds to reality, then it can be postulated that support for peace will rise if it can be shown to improve economic welfare; and it will decline if economic welfare is perceived to be diminished by peace.

The notion that attitudes to political questions, even those involving international relations, are influenced by material considerations is not new.

Nor is it confined to Marxist views of politics and economics. In Chapter 1 we discussed Professor Hirschman's analysis of the use made by Nazi Germany of commercial policy in turning other countries into political clients. This was done by promoting in these countries vested interests in association with Germany by offering their export sectors access on privileged terms to the lucrative, but highly protected, German market. In time, it became obvious to those engaged in trade with Germany that their continued prosperity depended on their government's support for Germany in international affairs. Powerful pro-German lobbies were thus created in many of Germany's trading partners, especially in the Balkan states.[1] Generalising from this experience Professor Hirschman says:

'If exports are concentrated in some region or industry, not only will the difficulty of adjustment in the case of loss of these exports weigh upon the decision of the governments, but these regions or industries will exert a powerful influence in favor of a "friendly" attitude toward the state to the imports of which they owe their existence.'

He then goes on to say:

'In the social pattern of each country there exist certain powerful groups the support of which is particularly valuable to a foreign country in its power policy; the foreign country will therefore try to establish commercial relations especially with these groups, in order that their voices will be raised in its favor.'[2]

The present definition of vested interest in peace and the description of the factors determining it may appear pessimistic. This approach apparently suggests that people's views are formed in response to their immediate and short-term material interests and that even their economic calculations are extremely myopic, because they ignore the benefits from the reduction in the defence burden which peace must ultimately make possible.

This is not necessarily the case. The public attitude to peace is obviously influenced by many factors – political, psychological and ideological as well as economic.[3] Peace may be fragile not because it conflicts with narrow economic interests within the countries concerned but rather because of the genuine political differences and the difficulties in finding compromises among conflicting claims. Under these circumstances, it makes sense to promote activities, economic and non-economic, which will increase the support for the peace process by demonstrating its benefits. It makes equally good sense to refrain from promotion of activities which make peace seem less palatable economically.

International trade theory shows that under most circumstances international transactions assumed voluntarily are Pareto-optimal. Collective and even individual welfare can be increased since the extra real income made available by the exchange could be distributed among the citizens of the country in question.[4] There is, however, no automatic mechanism which assures such redistribution and consequently it may well be that, while some gain from a given international transaction, other individuals lose. The effect of international transactions on vested interest in peace is therefore indeterminate, unless steps are taken either to compensate those whose welfare is adversely affected or to impose certain restrictions on international transactions between recent belligerents. In the second case, only transactions whose overall economic benefits are clearly discernible and which cause no economic injury to sections of the population that are politically articulate will be allowed.

The first alternative, that of compensating those injured by international transactions, appears to be ruled out. Its realisation would be handicapped by endless conceptual and administrative difficulties due to the problems involved in identifying and measuring injuries caused by international transactions. Moreover, it would be extremely difficult to devise equitable and administratively feasible methods of compensation. Finally, even if these difficulties could be overcome, there is no assurance that the measures would, in fact, be adopted. The second option – that is, allowing only those transactions which cause no injury to politically powerful groups – may thus be preferred in practice.

To clarify the above statement, it is useful to distinguish between two interest groups affected by international economic transactions: producers and consumers. Producers are those involved in the production of goods and services whose output is directly affected by the economic transactions under consideration – entrepreneurs, shareholders, employees, suppliers, sub-contractors and so on. Consumers are those who purchase the goods and services referred to above. Producer welfare rises when producer surplus goes up; that is, when revenues increase more than costs.[5] Consumer welfare in the present context is affected simply by price changes. When prices rise, consumer welfare declines; when prices decline, consumer welfare rises.

When considering the welfare effects of peace, the interests of the groups of producers and consumers do not necessarily coincide. For example, when the price of a given good goes up, producers of the good benefit and consumers lose. Decline in price may result in the curtailment of production and output: consumers benefit, producers lose and employment in the industry manufacturing the good may be curtailed.

If there were no possible divergence of interest between the groups discussed above there would be no need to bother about the determination of vested interest in peace. In this case, vested interest in peace would coincide, or at least have a one-to-one relationship, with conventional economic welfare. Transactions which can be shown to improve welfare , increase vested interest in peace and *vice versa*.[6]

How can conflict between the groups be resolved? In the present context, the answer is obvious – by the political process. Before proceeding with the discussion it is necessary, therefore, to rank the interest groups on the basis of their presumed political power. We assume that producer interests receive a higher priority from governments than consumer interests and that governments are particularly sensitive to employment. Specifically, we assume that the curtailment of employment, will simply not be tolerated.

The notion that producers' interests are dominant in the economy was argued as early as 1935, when Elmer E. Schattschneider stated that 'the consumers are at least as numerous as any other group in the society, but they have no organization to countervail the power of organized or monopolistic producers'.[7]

A similar argument was put forward by Vladimir O. Key in 1958: 'The lobbyists for electrical utilities, for example, are eternally on the job; the lobbyists for the consumers of this monopolistic service are ordinarily conspicuous by their absence.'[8]

Economist Mancur Olson, of the University of Maryland, took up this idea and developed it further. He argued that the organisation of producers and the fact that each industry comprises a relatively small number of firms makes them what he calls an 'intermediate' if not a privileged group 'with the political power that naturally and necessarily flows to those that control the business and property of the country'.[9] Consumers, on the other hand, form a large, unorganised group, a latent group which is 'organized only in special circumstances, but business interests are organized as a general rule'.[10]

Thomas Lachs, Director of the Consumers Association in Vienna, refers to governments embedding this 'producer dominance' consideration in their policies.[11] 'It is a fact that in capitalist societies ... governments have always developed their economic policy in close coordination with business interests. This is presumably a necessity and not even socialist governments have been able to act differently.'[12]

INITIATING TRADE BETWEEN RECENT BELLIGERENTS

Having outlined the relationship between vested interest in peace and the factors which determine it, we turn to the examination of specific international economic transactions – that is, international trade – with a view to evaluating their effect on vested interest in peace. The framework and the terminology used in analysing the effects of trade are both adapted from integration theory, which deals with the effects on welfare of reducing or abolishing tariffs and other barriers to the exchange of goods and services.[13]

Integration theory distinguishes between two effects of tariff reduction: trade creation and trade diversion. Trade creation takes place when, following the abolition of tariffs between A and B (after the establishment of a free trade area between them), A, instead of producing high-cost goods in which it has no comparative advantage, imports them from B. Trade diversion takes place when A stops importing goods from C, a low-cost producer whose imports are subjected to tariffs, and shifts to importing from B, a high-cost producer and a member of the free trade area. Trade creation is welfare enhancing while trade diversion has the effect of reducing welfare. Since the establishment of a free trade area results in both effects, it is impossible to state on *a priori* grounds whether the overall effect of integration is to increase or decrease welfare.[14]

The situation considered here differs from that of accepted integration theory in two important respects: integration theory deals with the case where two countries, A and B, grant each other concessions which are denied to the rest of the world. The present discussion focusses on the case where A and B agree to reduce discrimination between them and to treat each other in the same way that they treat the rest of the world.[15] As has been seen, preferences give rise to trade creation and trade diversion, which means welfare may either increase or decrease. Ending discrimination cannot decrease welfare, since it diversifies the sources of supply and increases the choice available to consumers.

Moreover, there is a basic difference in the treatment of welfare effects in the two cases. Integration theory focusses rightly and properly on consumption. A country's welfare is increased if it can consume more as a result of engaging in certain transactions. In the present case, alternative outcomes are not evaluated on the basis of their effect on overall welfare. Potential benefits and costs are valued on the basis of their impact on different groups of actors, whose welfare is weighed according to their political clout.

These considerations led us to formulate concepts similar to those used in integration theory in terms which make them more useful for the analysis of the relationship between trade and vested interest in peace. Before defining these concepts we outline briefly the analytical framework.

The framework of the following analysis is that of partial equilibrium which is commonly used by integration theorists and which is particularly useful for identification of the immediate impact of trade flows on the welfare of different economic actors. In the present case, the partial equilibrium framework is particularly appropriate because the analysis focusses on specific transactions which are unlikely to affect the entire economy. Furthermore, even the sum total of the bilateral transactions between past belligerents is unlikely to account for a substantial share of their total international transactions, at least in the short run. Macro-economic effects, for which a general equilibrium framework is more suitable, can therefore be ignored.

Reference is made, as before, to two countries, A and B (the past belligerents) and to a third country R (the rest of the world). The point of view is that of country A. The government of country A considers the likely effect of exporting a specific good on vested interest in peace in both countries. A and B are small countries; both are price takers. They trade with the rest of the world. International supply and demand schedules are infinitely elastic. Cost functions of two types are considered: increasing costs and decreasing costs.

In the first case, we assume that the product and factor markets are perfectly competitive. Aggregate cost functions are obtained by adding up horizontally the quantities produced by the individual enterprises at different prices.[16] In the second case, the presence of economies of scale is assumed to imply that, at most, one efficient plant is needed to supply the domestic market in A and B.[17]

The increasing marginal cost case is more suitable for the analysis of short-term effects – that is, the time span during which output capacity cannot be adjusted to meet changes in external conditions. In the long run, capacity can be expanded. Long-term average costs are likely to be horizontal in the absence of economies of scale and to be U-shaped if economies of scale exist.[18] It is therefore possible to treat the increasing and decreasing cost cases as reflecting the short and the long term respectively.

Before finishing with the preliminaries it may be helpful to consider transfer costs again. This term was used in Chapter 2 where it was not clearly defined. In the present chapter it is used extensively. The inclusion of transfer costs in the analysis turns out to have significant implications for the results. They are accordingly described in more detail. The term refers to the cost incurred in moving goods between producers located in one country and their foreign customers. Transfer costs include transportation costs and the excess of export over domestic marketing costs.[19] Tariffs are not considered part of transfer costs, although their inclusion would not affect the outcome, provided A is granted most-favoured-nation (MFN) status in B. In trade and integration theory, transfer costs are usually assumed to be equal to zero but, in the present case, transfer costs are crucially important.

Specifically, transfer costs between A and R and between B and R are assumed to be positive and equal and transfer costs between A and B to be negligible. Transfer costs between A and B are small partly because of physical distance, which affects the costs of transportation. There are, however, additional sources of cost savings. Many of the fixed and variable costs involved in international marketing can be reduced substantially. It may be possible, for example, to save on storage facilities and inventories. Double handling in shipping may be eliminated. In addition, customers may be served directly by the manufacturer, rather than by separate service organisations.

Physical proximity between trading partners is also likely to help reduce another important trade barrier – cultural distance. Cultural, like physical, distance gives rise to costs due to differences in language, in customs, in the ways of 'doing business' and, of course, in consumer tastes. The costs involved in overcoming cultural distance may constitute formidable trade barriers which could in many cases overwhelm the cost advantage due to the traditional 'comparative advantage'.[20] Between neighbouring countries these costs presumably decline over time, as experience accumulates and as the population, especially that section which lives along the borders of the two countries, acquires better knowledge of the conditions prevailing on the other side.[21]

There remain, of course, the man-made trade barriers represented by import duties and a host of trade restrictions and administrative regulations which hamper the flow of goods and services. These may or may not be reduced as part of the peace process. It is, however, possible to conclude that – other things being equal and unless A discriminates deliberately against B relative to R – physical proximity is likely to reduce trade barriers between A and B. The ending of belligerency between A and B consequently affects their bilateral trade potential much more if they are neighbours than if they have no common border.

Next, let us consider the different effects of opening up trade between neighbouring past belligerents. Distinction is made between the following trade categories: export diversion, import expansion, export expansion, export creation and output creation. The terms, as we shall see, have definite hierarchical connotations and refer to the rank ordering of the vested-interest-in-peace function.[22] As already indicated above, some of these terms are reminiscent of the terminology used in integration theory, which also deals with the lowering of trade barriers.

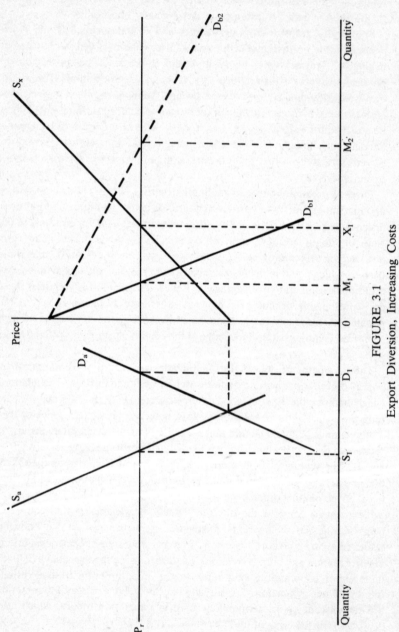

FIGURE 3.1
Export Diversion, Increasing Costs

EXPORT DIVERSION

Export diversion is illustrated in Figures 3.1 and 3.2. In Figure 3.1, which shows the rising cost case, the domestic market is shown separately from the world market. Domestic demand and supply schedules in A are shown on the left-hand side, where the quantity axis increases in value from right to left. S_a is A's supply curve (obtained by horizontally adding up the marginal cost

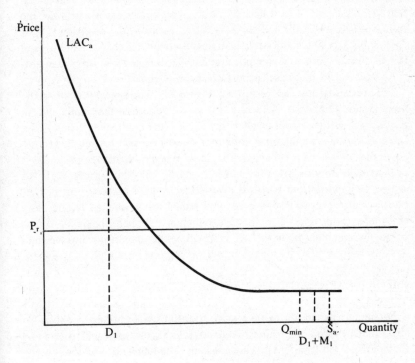

FIGURE 3.2
Export Diversion, Decreasing Costs

curves of all the producers in A who are competing against one another). S_x is A's excess supply curve: it represents A's offer of exports and is obtained by deducting for different prices the quantity demanded domestically from the quantity supplied. P_r stands for the price of the rest of the world. P_r is infinitely elastic.

Export diversion takes place when transfer costs are equal to zero. As long as A is barred from supplying B it produces S_1 and exports X_1 to R, selling the difference D_1 ($D_1 = S_1 - X_1$) in the domestic market.

B's excess demand curve (D_{b1}) is shown to the right of the price axis.[23] At world market price P_r, B imports M_1 from R. When imports from A are admitted into B, they can vary from zero to M_1. A's exporters, however, are likely to have an edge over R because of the physical proximity between the countries. If this edge allows them to shed their price even by an infinitesimal amount, A's exporters could capture a high share of B's import market. In that case, A's exports to R decline. At the margin, A's exports to R decline from X_1 to $X_1 - M_1$. The amount $X_1 - M_1$ represents export diversion from R to B. If B's excess demand curve intersects S_x to the right of X_1, like D_{b2}, and A sells all its exports to B, the price remains P_r, B imports X_1 from A and $M_2 - X_1$ from R. In that case, export diversion is equal to A's total exports.

The decreasing cost case is shown in Figure 3.2. World price P_r is above the point where long-run average costs, LAC_a, reaches the minimum. A produces S_a (which is not smaller than Q_{min} – the minimum efficient plant size). At S_a long-run marginal costs (not shown) equal P_r. A sells D_1 ($D_1 < S_a$) in the domestic market and $S_a - D_1$ in R. When trade between A and B is permitted, B imports M_1 from A. $M_1 < \max S_a - D_1$, M_o, where M_o is B's pre-peace imports from R. M_1 is diverted from other markets provided A, due to its proximity to B, has some infinitesimal cost advantage over R. Note that this outcome depends on LAC_a's minimum point being below P_r. If P_r is below the minimum point of LAC_a, A will neither export nor produce and A's (as well as B's) consumption will be imported from R.

IMPORT EXPANSION AND EXPORT EXPANSION

For import expansion to take place, transfer costs must be positive. To simplify the analysis we assume that fixed transfer costs are equal to zero and that variable unit transfer costs are constant. The following notation is used:

P_a = domestic market price in A
t = unit transfer costs
$P_r - t$ = export receipts per unit exported to R
$P_r + t$ = cost per unit imported from R

Consider first the case where marginal costs rise. The effects of introducing trade between A and B in this case are shown in Figure 3.3. Transfer costs, although positive, do not prevent A from exporting to R. A's exporters receive $P_r - t$, which equals the domestic price in A (P_a). The quantity

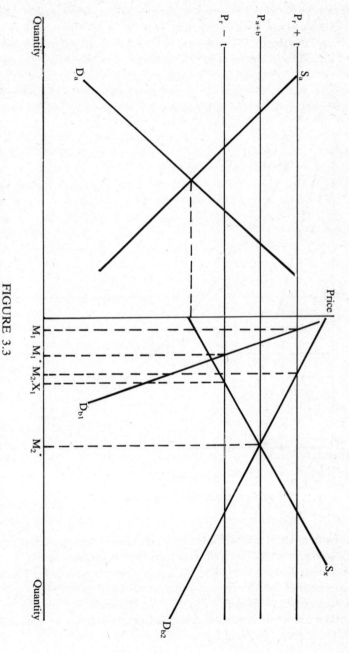

FIGURE 3.3
Import Expansion and Export Expansion, Increasing Costs

exported is X_1. If A's exports are admitted into B, whose excess demand is D_{b1}, exports will be diverted from R to B. Total exports remain at X_1, although the share of R in A's exports declines from 100 per cent to $(X_1 - M_1^*)/X_1$. The situation from B's point of view, however, has changed. Instead of importing M_1 from R at the price of $P_r + t$, B now imports M_1^* at a lower price, P_r-t. We label the case where export prices and receipts remain unchanged in A, in spite of the increase in B's imports, import expansion.

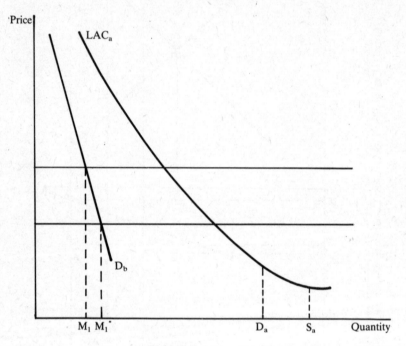

FIGURE 3.4
Import Expansion, Decreasing Costs

The situation is different if B's excess demand is large enough to divert all A's exports from R. This is the case when B's demand schedule is D_{b2}. Here, B's imports increase from M_2 to M_2^* and A's exports increase from X_1 to M_2^*. Prices received by A's exporters rise from $P_r - t$ to P_{a+b} and prices paid by B's consumers decline from $P_r - t$ to P_{a+b}. To distinguish the last case from the previous one where A's export prices and quantities remained unchanged, we label it export expansion.

The decreasing cost version of import expansion is shown in Figure 3.4. Before peace A produces S_a, sells D_a in the domestic market and exports $S_a - D_a$. B imports M_1 at the price $P_r + t$. When imports from A are admitted B imports M_1^* ($M_1^* > M_1$), paying $P_r - t$ ($P_r - t < P_r + t$).[24]

EXPORT CREATION AND OUTPUT CREATION

Export creation is the decreasing cost equivalent of export expansion. The reason for the difference in the labels is demonstrated in Figure 3.5. Here, the

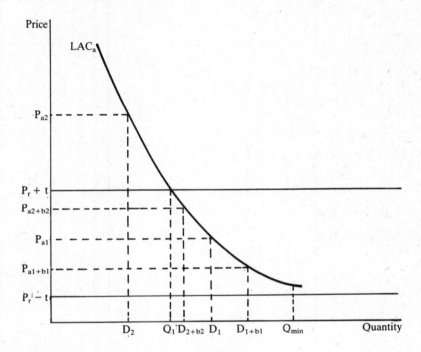

FIGURE 3.5
Export and Output Creation

minimum cost point of LAC_a is above $P_r - t$. A can therefore under no circumstances export to R. Whether production takes place depends on whether domestic demand intersects with LAC_a to the left or to the right of Q_1. If the curves intersect to the right of Q_1 at D_1, A's consumers can be charged a price P_{a1} ($P_{a1} < P_r + t$, where $P_r + t$ is the import price).[25] A's costs

TABLE 3.1

Different Trade Effects and their Impact on Vested Interest in Peace

	Export diversion	Import expansion	Export expansion	Export creation	Output creation
Costs					
Production	rise decline	rise decline	rise	decline	decline
Transfer	0	+	+	+	+
Welfare effects					
Consumers in A	0	0	-	+	+
Consumers in B	0	+	0	+	+
Producers in A	0	0	+	+	+
Other effects in A[a]	none	none	export, output rise	export, output rise	new investment
VIP[b] rank	1	2	3	4	5

[a] With the exception of export diversion, output and employment increase in B's industries manufacturing complementary goods and services. The ranking assumes that government policy in B prevents import competition from affecting employment adversely.
[b] Vested interest in peace

will move along the declining LAC_a curve. The cost of producing for both markets at D_{1+b1} will be P_{a1+b1}. The opening of B's market transforms A from a domestic into an international producer. This is why this case is labelled export creation.

Finally, consider output creation, which is also illustrated in Figure 3.5. Here, domestic demand (not shown) and LAC_a intersect to the left of Q_1 at D_2 ($P_{a2} > P_r + t$). Imports are less costly than domestic production. If demand at A plus B intersects LAC_a to the right of Q_1 at D_{2+b2}, then the opening of B's market is a condition not only for exports but also for production in A – hence the label output creation.

EFFECT OF TRADE ON WELFARE AND VESTED INTEREST IN PEACE

The different trade effects are summarised in Table 3.1, which ranks the effects according to their impact on welfare in the two countries and on vested interest in peace. The ranking scheme proposed here is based on immediate or first-order effects only. When considering the effects of a transaction, only the impact on employment, profits, price of output and so on of the enterprises immediately affected are taken into account. Secondary effects, that is, the effects on suppliers and on other sectors, are ignored.

Export diversion has no welfare effects. Consumers do not pay lower prices and producers do not receive higher revenues. Consequently, the vested-interest-in-peace ranking of export diversion is necessarily low, as are the costs of dissociation. Note that this conclusion holds regardless of the volume of trade diverted from R to B. Even if all of B's imports are switched to A and even if B becomes A's major customer when trade between the two countries is allowed, there are only infinitesimal gains in consumers' and producers' welfare in the two countries. This conclusion holds regardless of whether marginal costs are rising or declining. It is explained by the fact that although A and B refrained from trading with each other before the conclusion of peace, their economies were in fact inter-connected via their trade with R. When trade is opened up there are no additional welfare gains to be made.

When import expansion takes place, consumers in B benefit because they obtain more imports at lower prices than before. The welfare of consumers and producers in A remains unchanged, since the total value of exports from A remains fixed, regardless of whether marginal costs of production rise or decline. Since nobody's welfare is adversely affected by import expansion, it gets a higher vested-interest-in-peace rank than export diversion .

Export expansion affects the welfare of consumers in A and B and of producers in A. While consumer welfare in B increases ($P_{a+b} < P_r + t$), that of A's consumers declines ($P_{a+b} > P_r - t$). A's producers receive a higher price for a larger output – their welfare rises, of course. Bearing in mind the earlier discussion concerning the relative political power of consumers and producers, and recalling that B's consumers benefit, we conclude that export expansion has an overall positive effect on vested interest in peace (in both countries), even though one sector of A's population is hurt. Export expansion ranks third on the vested-interest-in-peace ranking scale.[26]

Export and import expansion require an increase in production capacity. Consequently, costs of dissociation may be substantive, due to both the higher economic gains to the parties involved and the investments required to establish the larger production capacity, some of which might not have alternative uses.

Export creation and output creation have positive welfare effects on all the relevant actors. Unit costs fall as a result of moving along the declining cost curve. Producers in A need not pass on all their cost savings to the consumers, but even if they charge prices which equate marginal revenues with marginal costs in both countries, they have to reduce prices to sell their higher output. Consumers in A and B will consequently enjoy net gains.[27]

Output creation offers additional benefits. In the first place, producers in A and consumers in A and B benefit from expansion of output and reduction in costs as in the case of export creation. Employment is increased as in the case of export expansion. The effect of output creation on vested interest in peace is expected to be greater than that of export creation. While both have a positive impact on the economic welfare of all the relevant actors in both countries, output creation is the only case where peace makes it possible to establish an industry whose viability depends on the existence of trade between A and B. No other situation discussed so far has such a clear-cut and easily identifiable positive impact.

Analysis of the costs of dissociation in the last two categories shows that, in cases involving output and export creation, the loss per unit of projected sales, if trade is disrupted, is even greater than in cases of import or export expansion. Curtailment of production following dissociation in these cases means that economies of scale are going to be lost. The production facilities of the industry in question may have to be closed down altogether if the higher unit costs, due to smaller output, exceed the price of competing imports.

Thus, without having to measure and compare the welfare of the different actors, while making only a single and hopefully plausible assumption about the relative political clout of the relevant actors, it is possible to rank the different trade effects according to their expected impact on vested interest in peace.[28]

POLICY IMPLICATIONS

While the grouping of the transactions according to their trade effects and to their impact on vested interest in peace, as outlined in the last section, has implications for policy making, no single policy is necessarily indicated. Moreover, adoption of the ranking scheme outlined in Table 3.1 is consistent with different policies ranging from complete *laissez faire* through to detailed intervention in individual transactions. None of the transactions is welfare reducing in either A or B when welfare is considered in the conventional sense of the word. Export diversion has neither positive nor negative conventional welfare effects. With the exception of import expansion, which increases welfare only in B, all the remaining transactions enhance welfare in both countries, since they follow the elimination of discriminatory restrictions and not the institution of discrimination (as is the case when two countries establish a free trade area or grant each other preferences). Thus if A's government believes in *laissez faire*, it might decide to refrain from interfering in or influencing the decisions of domestic firms concerning exports to B. In this case, there is no need to distinguish among the different kinds of transactions discussed above. Firms in A will presumably make their own calculations and will decide whether and how much to export to B on the basis of expected prices, sales, costs, risk *et cetera*. On the other hand, even a *laissez faire*-oriented government in B will restrict those imports which reduce producer welfare because of their adverse effects on vested interest in peace.[29] It will, however, be indifferent to those imports which do not compete with local production, regardless of the category to which they belong.

Governments may decide to adopt a more interventionist policy and to discriminate among the different categories of transactions. Such discrimination could be justified on the grounds of (i) the contribution to vested interest in peace, (ii) the risk assumed by the enterprises engaged in trade and (iii) the effect on the cost of dissociation.

The contribution to vested interest in peace of the different transactions was discussed above and need not be repeated here. Since there is no necessary correspondence between private gain and vested interest in peace, the government could help to change the relative attractiveness of the transactions, offering higher incentives for export creation than for export expansion, for example. If this policy is adopted, the government could be guided by ranking schemes of the kind outlined in Table 3.1.[30]

Similar considerations apply to the treatment of risk. Obviously, economic transactions with a past belligerent will be viewed as more risky by individual enterprises than trading with established customers. Some of these risks emanate from lack of knowledge and information about the market. In time, these particular risks are likely to disappear. When economic transactions are in their initial stages, however, they may constitute a barrier. The ranking scheme of Table 3.1 offers a guide as to the relative riskiness of these transactions. Export diversion and import expansion, for example, are not very risky; when transfer costs are negligible, firms in country A are indifferent as to whether to export to B or to R. Similarly, risks are small even if transfer costs are positive, when the free-on-board (f.o.b.) price charged in the different markets is the same and shipments can be shifted between B and R in both directions without incurring losses. Export expansion involves higher risks since it is likely to require additional resources, including labour and possibly investment in production facilities. Export creation is still more risky. It requires, in addition to the above, commitment of resources to the development of the export marketing – a function with which the enterprises in question are unfamiliar by definition.[31]

Output creation is more risky than export creation, since it pertains to the manufacture of new products which must be marketed in both A and B if they are to be internationally competitive. The scheme presented in Table 3.1 is also useful for ranking transactions according to their costs of dissociation, discussed at length in Chapter 2.

Clearly, the transactions discussed in the last two sections contribute differently to the costs of dissociation and hence to dependence of A on B and vice versa. Their ranking according to their impact on dependence is in fact the same as the ranking according to risk. Transactions which were here identified as riskier from A's point of view are also costlier to annul. Thus establishment in A of an industry which depends for its survival on exports to B is riskier than shifting existing exports from R to B. The higher risks are caused by the lack of alternative markets in the first case and by the potential bankruptcy faced by A's enterprises if exports to B are discontinued.[32] Risks are higher still when A depends on B not only for markets but also for inputs, as in the case of joint ventures.[33]

The policy instruments likely to be used by the government to promote vested interest in peace, to handle risk and to avoid excessive dependence are quite different. In the first case, fiscal measures, including subsidies, grants and tax relief, may be the most appropriate. In the second case, insurance schemes may be preferred. In the third case, administrative intervention may be deemed necessary. In all cases, however, the same information is required by the decision maker. The concepts developed in this chapter should be helpful in identifying the type of information needed and in evaluating its usefulness in the context of initiating trade between past belligerents.

The effect of imports from A on production in B has been incompletely treated thus far. The negative effect of import competition on vested interest in peace was assumed away by stating that transactions which will hurt the politically powerful producers will be disallowed. At first glance, it appears that if A and B grant each other MFN status, the problem is resolved. Governments can be assumed to establish import regulations which provide import-competing sectors with a degree of protection consistent with the 'national interest'. Note, however, that B's pre-peace commercial policy is presumably designed to give domestic producers an acceptable degree of protection vis-à-vis R's producers. Since the latter are handicapped by transfer costs, the degree of protection given to B's marginal producers against imports from R may be insufficient to protect them against imports from A. Consequently, if B's producers are to enjoy the same degree of protection against A's as against R's producers, higher tariffs may have to be charged on imports from A. If A's government wishes to promote vested interest in peace in B it will accept some degree of discrimination against its exporters, even though this entails departure from the MFN principle.[34]

To summarise, our analysis has shown that the economic effects of transition from war to peace are not confined to the gains which can be derived from reducing the defence burden, on the one hand, and to the costs involved in scaling down the defence industries and re-allocation of employment and investment in the economy, on the other. Substantial gains may be derived from bilateral transactions between the past belligerents and from the reorientation of their economies towards each other.

The potential for economic cooperation between past belligerents who happen to be neighbours is likely to be greater and more varied than the potential for exchange of goods and services between any other pair of countries. The potential gains from 'normal' trade between them is limited, especially if the countries in question are small and if they have been extensively engaged in international trade prior to concluding peace between them. In that case, even if substantial trade is diverted from third countries, it is unlikely to affect relative costs by more than a fraction. The real prizes should be looked for elsewhere, not in the two countries' existing trade, but rather among those goods and services which have hitherto been considered as non-tradeable – that is, those goods and services which were either not produced at all or, if produced, were not exported due to the high cost of international transfer. It is the expansion of the tradeables sector which may well be the source of most substantial gain from economic intercourse between past belligerents.

A POSSIBLE EXAMPLE

The usefulness of the concepts introduced in this chapter is illustrated by a concrete example involving the Egyptian-Israeli peace process.[35] The example considered here pertains to the cement industry, whose economic and technological characteristics qualify it as a possible candidate for economic cooperation between the two countries.

Cement is a bulky product whose value relative to its weight is low. It is consequently not usually transported over long distances. The production process is subject to significant economies of scale and the minimum size of an efficient plant is large. When a new plant is built, the addition to a small country's production capacity can be quite substantial. Thus temporary excess capacity is often found in a country or region where a new plant was recently completed. Since the production process is highly capital-intensive and since marginal costs are low, it pays to produce at full capacity and to export the surplus, as long as prices exceed marginal costs. This alternative is preferred to production at less than full capacity, which raises unit costs substantially. Exports are only temporary as a rule, since capacity is designed to take care of 'normal' domestic demand. As domestic demand expands, exports are first reduced and finally discontinued. If and when domestic demand expands further, temporary imports are required to take care of it, since expansion implies substantial increase in capacity that cannot be effected at short notice.

The timing of new investments and their volume is rather tricky, particularly in small countries, because of the bulkiness of the investment. Thus small countries are likely to depend more on foreign trade in cement than large countries. Dependence on foreign trade in cement is undesirable because of the high cost of transportation coupled with substantial uncertainties associated with supplies, markets and prices.

Cooperation between Egypt and Israel in the cement industry could be beneficial to both countries in several respects. If trade barriers to cement are eliminated, the two countries can form a single market, thus benefiting from economies of scale and being less dependent on erratic markets and suppliers.

As of the end of 1980, both Egypt (with six plants) and Israel (with three) have been rather short of cement and both countries have been planning to increase their production capacity over the coming years. The establishment of economic relations between the two countries poses some interesting questions regarding the location of Israel's fourth plant. The plant could conceivably be located in Egypt rather than Israel, since Egypt enjoys a considerable cost advantage in energy, which is used intensively in the manufacture of cement. Cost savings in energy could compensate for the higher transportation costs incurred in shipping cement over longer distances. Tentative calculations indicate that a plant located in Egypt could compete with an Israeli plant in the Israeli market if the former could obtain gas at a price representing a 30-35 per cent discount over the cost of energy obtained from coal imported by Israel. A transaction of this kind is conceivably profitable for Egypt, considering the alternative uses for its gas.

Assuming that this is indeed the case, let us see how some of the concepts developed earlier can be used to gain additional insights into the possible effects of the transactions on the two countries.

The cement project described above obviously belongs to the export-creation category. Peaceful relations with Israel make it possible to establish in Egypt a potentially welfare-enhancing new export industry which will earn urgently-needed foreign exchange. If prices are competitive, consumer welfare in Israel, too, will be raised.[36] Other factors must, however, be examined as well. Consider the nature and extent of mutual dependence which the project generates. Egyptian plants each employing over one hundred people become dependent on a single foreign market. Bearing in mind the high transportation costs, it is unlikely that alternative export markets will be profitable. As for the Israelis, they depend on a single foreign supplier for about one-quarter of their cement, which is an important material in the construction industry. If supplies are discontinued, alternative sources are bound to be more expensive. Both sides should consider additional risks. If Egyptian domestic demand rises, will prices be raised or supplies diverted? If demand in Israel slackens, will the Israelis reduce domestic purchases or will they rather reduce their imports?

Questions such as these inevitably surface whenever a bulky investment project is being considered. In the present context, however, it is not only the economic welfare of those affected by the decision which is at stake; the peace process, too, may be affected, since it is the recent enemy which appears responsible for both the gains from cooperation and the losses caused by disruption. Clearly, no government can be indifferent to either possibility. It is for this reason that governments play an important role in establishing the rules which govern the volume and form of bilateral transactions between recent belligerents.

NOTES AND REFERENCES

1. See Hirschman, *National Power and the Structure of Foreign Trade, op. cit.*, ch. 2.

2. *Ibid.*, p. 29.

3. See Raymond Aron, *The Century of Total War* (Boston: Beacon Press, 1966) ch. 3, for a detailed discussion of the relationship between economic factors and attitude towards war in Europe.

4. On this point, see Kenneth J. Arrow, *Social Choice and Individual Values* (New Haven and London: Yale University Press, 1951) ch. 4.

5. The producers include several sub-groups which must share the welfare gains accruing to the entire group. We assume here that, when the group benefits from net gains, it shares them in a way which raises the welfare of each sub-group.

6. Alternatively, if it could be assumed that the 'compensation principle' would in fact be applied and that those injured by competition from abroad would be compensated, vested interest in peace would be equated with economic welfare also in this case. If compensation cannot be guaranteed there is no necessary correspondence between vested interest in peace and conventional welfare gains.

7. See Elmer E. Schattschneider, *Politics, Pressures and the Tariff* (New York: Prentice Hall, 1935), cited in Mancur Olson Jr, *The Logic of Collective Action: Public Goods and the Theory of Groups* (Cambridge, Mass.: Harvard University Press, 1965).

8. See Vladimir O. Key Jr, *Politics, Parties and Pressure Groups*, 4th ed. (New York: Crowell, 1958) p. 166.

9. See Olson, *op. cit.*, p. 128.

10. *Ibid.*

11. Such considerations have been used in studies on trade policy, for example Richard Blackhurst, Nicolas Marian and Jan Tumlir, *Trade Liberalization, Protectionism and Interdependence*, GATT Studies in International Trade No. 5 (Geneva: GATT Secretariat, 1977) pp. 32-33, and in many studies on regulation, for example J.A. Wilson, 'The Politics of Regulation', in J.W. McKie (ed.), *Social Responsibility and the Business Predicament* (Washington: Brookings Institution, 1974) and G. Doron, *The Smoking Paradox: Public Regulations in the Cigarette Industry* (Cambridge, Mass.: Abt Books, 1979).

12. See Thomas Lachs' comment on Conrad Blyth's paper 'The Interaction between Collective Bargaining and Government Policies in Selected Member Countries', in *Collective Bargaining and Government Policies*, proceedings of a conference held in Washington, United States, 10-13 July 1978 (Paris: OECD Secretariat, 1979) p. 97.

13. See Jacob Viner, *The Customs Union Issue* (New York: Carnegie Endowment for International Peace, 1950) and Bela Balassa, *Theory of Economic Integration* (Homewood, Illinois: Richard Irwin, 1962).

14. For a detailed survey of the literature dealing with the conditions under which integration leads to welfare gains or losses, see Richard G. Lipsey, 'The Theory of Customs Unions: a General Survey', *Economic Journal*, London, September 1960, pp. 496-513, and Melvyn B. Krauss, 'Recent Developments in Customs Union Theory: an Interpretative Survey', *Journal of Economic Literature*, Nashville, Tennessee, June 1972. For a discussion of the modern versions of the theory, see Eytan Berglas, 'Preferential Trading Theory: the n Commodity Case', *Journal of Political Economy*, Chicago, April 1979, pp. 315-31.

15. They may be viewed as reducing infinite tariffs imposed on trade between them to the level applied to the rest of the world. There may be limits, however, to the elimination of discrimination

between past belligerents seeking to promote vested interest in peace.

16. In fact, aggregate cost functions are likely to rise at a higher rate than individual cost functions, if we take into account the likelihood that as all individual enterprises in a given industry seek to expand output they will run into supply bottlenecks not encountered by an individual enterprise which decides to expand.

17. Recall that A and B are small countries.

18. The shapes, however, could be modified by the macro-effects mentioned in note 16 above.

19. For a discussion of the difference between domestic and export marketing costs, see Hirsch, 'An International Trade and Investment Theory of the Firm', *Oxford Economic Papers*, Oxford, July 1976, pp. 258-70.

20. Indeed, writers such as Staffan Burenstam Linder, of the Stockholm School of Economics, advanced the proposition that trade between countries declines as the cultural distance (measured by difference in per capita income) increases. This proposition conflicts with expectations derived from the Heckscher-Ohlin model. See Burenstam Linder, *An Essay on Trade and Transformation* (New York: John Wiley, 1961). For an attempt to reconcile the two models, see Arad and Hirsch, 'Determinants of Trade Flows and Choice of Trade Partners: Reconciling the Heckscher-Ohlin and Burenstam Linder Models of International Trade', *Weltwirtschaftliches Archiv*, Kiel, vol. 117, no. 2, 1981, pp. 276-97.

21. The above proposition is supported by the mounting evidence of large-scale smuggling taking place between Israel and Egypt following the signing of the peace treaty.

22. In the study by Alfred Tovias, *Tariff Preferences in Mediterranean Diplomacy* (London: Macmillan, for the Trade Policy Research Centre, 1977), a similar term, export trade diversion, is used to describe the effect of preference agreements on the direction of exports. The policy instrument in Dr Tovias' model is tariff reduction. In this case it is removal of discrimination. The welfare effects are consequently different.

23. The excess demand curve is derived (similarly to the excess supply curve) by deducting for each price the quantity supplied domestically from the quantity demanded.

24. A similar case is discussed in W.M. Corden, 'Economies of Scale and Customs Union Theory', *Journal of Political Economy*, 1972, pp. 465-75. Here the gains from expanding output of products enjoying economies of scale are labelled 'cost reduction effects'. In Professor Corden's example, gains from cost reduction may be counter-balanced by losses due to trade-suppression effects 'which take place when a dear source replaces a cheap one with the formation of a customs union'.

25. The actual price in A will depend on the extent to which A's producer-monopolist is able to exercise his pricing power.

26. Obviously, if consumers are politically more powerful, export expansion might be ranked lower than export diversion, which offers no welfare gains.

27. Analytically, output creation is similar to Professor Corden's trade suppression. The difference between the overall welfare effects of output creation (which is positive) and trade suppression (which is negative) is due to the presence of transfer costs which are non-existent in Professor Corden's model.

28. Note, however, that the ranks might be changed in specific cases when information about the second-order effects is available. Note, also, that the scheme ignores effects on producers in B, which may be positive if the latter produce complementary goods, or negative if they manufacture competing products.

29. Actually, competing imports, which are assumed here to have negative effects on vested interest in peace, are precisely those transactions which integration theory labels 'trade creating' and which are regarded as welfare enhancing. This conflict between the policy implications of integration theory and the present approach is explained by the assumptions about the political

predominance of producer over consumer interests in the government decision-making process.

30. Note, however, the cautionary remark in note 28 above.

31. Note that risk and vested-interest-in-peace considerations do not produce identical ranks. Export expansion has a higher risk than the vested-interest-in-peace rank.

32. B also assumes risks in relying on supplies from A. The risks and the costs involved are not the same in both countries. In most cases, the risk assumed by B is lower.

33. These risks, however, are neutralised to a certain extent due to the dependence of B on A for markets for the input it supplies to the joint venture.

34. Alternatively, the MFN principle could be reformulated on a cost-insurance-freight (c.i.f.) basis, thus allowing A's and R's exporters to compete on an equal footing in B. The discriminatory advantage which transfer costs confer on some traders is discussed in Alexander J. Yeats, 'Tariff Valuation, Transport Costs and the Establishment of Trade Preferences among Developing Countries', *World Development,* vol. 8, no.1, 1980, pp. 129-36. Dr Yeats argues that c.i.f.-based tariff valuation often discriminates against the developing countries and suggests that some of this discrimination can be removed by changing the valuation basis from c.i.f. to f.o.b. This suggestion is in line with the approach suggested here.

35. Based on a preliminary study by Simcha Bahiri, of the Israel Institute of Business Research at Tel Aviv University.

36. Recall that the alternative is to build a more expensive plant in Israel.

CHAPTER 4

Cooperative Ventures between Recent Enemies

The analysis in Chapter 3 focussed on bilateral transactions facilitated by the opening up of borders between recent belligerents. Trade in goods belonging to the export- and import-diversion categories, which, prior to peace, were exported to or imported from the rest of the world, is switched, following peace, to the new trading partner. Goods in the export- and output-creation categories, which before peace were not exported at all, are similarly traded only between the recent enemies. In these categories, trade with the rest of the world is ruled out because of high transfer costs.

The transactions considered in Chapter 3 have an additional characteristic: they involve international exchange between producers located in one country and buyers located in another – that is, mutually complementary relationships between partners. Division of tasks, direct foreign investment and other types of cooperation between producers in both A and B, which involve symmetrical relationships between partners, do not figure in these transactions.

COOPERATIVE VENTURES

This chapter introduces an additional type of transaction between past belligerents and examines its economic effects: the cooperative venture – a new economic enterprise which, in order to be internationally competitive, depends on inputs from both A and B.

The analytical framework used here, as in Chapter 3, is that of a three-country world consisting of two small countries, A and B, which had until recently been at war with each other, and a third large country R (the rest of the world). It is assumed that international transactions involve positive transfer costs, which consist of the difference between the cost of delivering goods or services to domestic and foreign buyers. It is further assumed that transfer costs involving neighbouring countries are smaller than those between distant countries.

Cooperative ventures are defined as recurrent transactions between two or more enterprises whose profitability depends on cooperation between them. Cooperative ventures become international when the enterprises under consideration are located in different countries. The following example illustrates the conditions which are conducive to the establishment of international cooperative ventures.

Consider a product whose production costs are denoted as follows:

$$S_j = S_{1j} + S_{2j}$$

where S_j is the unit cost of the finished product in country j (j = A, B, R) and S_{1j} and S_{2j} represent the unit costs of the two inputs used in the production process in one of the countries.[1] S_{1j} and S_{2j} could be primary inputs such as labour, capital or natural resources. They could also be intermediate goods or intangibles such as skills, management, technological or marketing know-how.

Let us assume that a comparison between domestic and import costs in A and B yields the following relationships:

$$S_a > S_r + t \text{ and } S_b > S_r + t$$

that is, domestic production costs in both A and B exceed import costs from R, which are $S_r + t$. Let us further assume that a cooperative venture, using factors of production from both A and B (say, input 1 from A and input 2 from B, yielding unit production costs denoted by S_{ab}), can successfully compete with imports; that is,

$$S_{ab} = S_{1a} + S_{2b} < S_r + t$$

Then the product is a suitable candidate for import substitution in either A or B, provided enterprises in the two countries cooperate in its production. In this case, the required cooperation goes beyond the commitment of the two countries to open the market for each other's goods. Cooperation, in turn, implies that enterprises in the two countries must coordinate their activities.

In a sense, cooperative ventures are an extension of the output-creation category, introduced in Chapter 3. Both encompass activities which are economically feasible only if transactions between A and B are allowed. Cooperative ventures, however, offer important advantages over and above those inherent in the simple international exchange of goods and services. It has been noted already that none of the transactions discussed in Chapter 2 makes it possible to increase the list of exportables from either A or B to the rest of the world (R). When cooperative ventures are introduced this limitation no longer holds. Cooperative ventures thus facilitate expanding not only the range of tradeable goods but also the number of potential markets where both existing and new tradeables can be sold.

Information about the characteristics of the goods or services supplied by enterprises located in A and B to the cooperative venture might enable us to predict the nature of the relationship between the enterprises. For this purpose it is useful to employ the terminology used by John H. Dunning, of the University of Reading in the United Kingdom, to distinguish between two types of advantage enjoyed by enterprises competing in the international markets – 'location' and 'ownership' advantage.[2]

Location advantage, as the term suggests, derives from the place where the activity takes place. Natural resources and the abundance of production factors, such as capital or labour, as well as the availability and quality of infra-structure (transportation, communication services *et cetera*), are typically referred to as sources of locational advantage. Government policies such as taxes, tariffs or subsidies may also be considered as contributing to this form of advantage. The advantages conferred by a specific location are, as a rule, available on essentially equal terms to anybody choosing the location under consideration.[3]

Ownership advantage is, by contrast, firm-specific. It derives from specific knowledge developed or otherwise acquired by the firm – production know-how, product or market information, management know-how, patents, trademarks or other types of proprietary knowledge which can be used to yield profits and which can be effectively withheld from potential competitors.

Location advantage is realised through trade; it is the source of comparative advantage familiar from international trade theory. Its source is abundant endowment of natural resources or of other production factors, such as labour or capital, whose relative abundance in a particular country enables it to produce internationally-competitive goods.[4] Ownership advantage can be exploited internationally by trade or, alternatively, by direct investment. The form in which ownership advantage is realised depends on whether the home country or the prospective host country enjoys an advantage in the supply of the complementary factors of production (constituting the location advantage) which must be combined with the proprietary inputs provided by the firm. If the costs of these location-based inputs are lower in the home market than in the foreign markets, the firm will exploit its ownership advantage by exporting. If the host country provides a less expensive source of inputs, foreign direct investment will consequently take place. The rich literature concerned with international investment, multinational enterprises and the internationalisation of the firm amply illustrates the ways in which location and ownership advantage are combined by enterprises engaged in multinational operations.[5]

These studies, however, are rarely concerned with ownership and control. It is usually assumed that the firm possessing the ownership advantage owns and controls activities which transform its proprietary knowledge, together with the inputs obtained from the most advantageous location, into marketable goods and services. This, however, is not the only possible outcome, since the proprietary knowledge giving rise to the ownership advantage can, under certain circumstances, be transferred to other firms by way of patent sales, licensing, know-how agreements, management contracts, franchising and the like.[6]

DOMINANCE

International cooperative ventures were defined in the last section as frameworks for cooperation between enterprises located in two countries.[7] Cooperation is dictated by the nature of the production function, which consists of two or more stages or inputs. The need for cooperation as such does not determine its exact form. Cooperation could be in the form of arm's-length transactions between entirely independent entities. This form would prevail in those cases where the output of the different stages consists of a commodity or intermediate good supplied through the market. If, however, the output is specific and its only or major use is as an input for a single final product, then the coordination required between the two stages is unlikely to be achieved through the market.[8] In this case, contractual or other types of binding relationship might have to be established between enterprises in the two countries.

The implications of the direct foreign investment model to the present case are straightforward. The cooperative venture will tend to be controlled or dominated by the party possessing the ownership advantage. The direct foreign investment referred to above is, in fact, a special case of a cooperative venture – where the firm in country A possesses an ownership advantage and the firm in country B possesses a locational advantage. In this case, the country A firm can presumably acquire the inputs it requires from B in the market provided both firms are allowed by their governments to transact freely. If, on the other hand, a firm in country B wants to obtain the inputs which the country A firm owns, it cannot do so by using the market mechanism, since the country A firm advantage is, by definition, firm-specific. We may conclude, therefore, on the basis of *a priori* reasoning that in cases such as the one just described – that is, where A has an ownership advantage and B a locational advantage – the cooperative venture will be dominated by the country with the ownership advantage.

This outcome is particularly likely to prevail in those cases where the output of the cooperative venture is destined for export to third countries. In this case it is unlikely that output will be limited to the declining portion of the average cost curve. When output, however, is intended to replace imports in A and B (output creation), B's location advantage could take the form of a natural monopoly brought into being by the small size of the combined domestic markets of A and B, which in many cases will not justify the establishment of more than just one single plant of efficient minimum size. In cases such as these, B's locational advantage could be transformed into an ownership advantage. This can be accomplished by prohibiting foreign firms from controlling natural monopolies, a policy commonly adopted even in market economies, where the private sector predominates.[9]

The *raison d'être* of cooperative ventures need not be A's ownership and B's location advantage. Cooperative ventures can make economic sense with different types of advantages originating in A and B. Altogether four such types are possible:

(a) A has ownership advantage, B has location advantage (A_oB_l);
(b) A has ownership advantage, B has ownership advantage (A_oB_o);
(c) A has location advantage, B has ownership advantage (A_lB_o); and
(d) A has location advantage, B has location advantage (A_lB_l).

A_oB_l was discussed above. Cooperative ventures of this type will tend to be dominated by A, while A_lB_o will tend to be dominated by B. A_oB_o and A_lB_l represent more difficult cases. The information about the production characteristics provided in the symbols A_lB_l and A_oB_o alone is insufficient as a basis for predicting whether A or B will dominate these cooperative ventures. For this purpose more precise information about the specifics of the case in question is required. The country enjoying a relative (rather than absolute) ownership advantage in the first case and relative location advantage in the second will tend to dominate the cooperative venture in question.

The form in which cooperation between the different countries takes place and the identity of the party which dominates cooperative ventures is, of course, not unimportant. The large literature on the multinational enterprise clearly indicates that the interested parties, namely governments, business organisations, labour unions, consumers and so on, are not indifferent to the form in which domestic and foreign interests interact.[10] The form of this interaction and its control is of even greater importance in the context of peacemaking, where highly sensitive political issues are hardly separable from purely economic ones.

The literature on multinational enterprises suggests that foreign domination of national enterprises by foreign-owned or foreign-controlled enterprises is often disapproved of in the host country.[11] Foreign multinationals are alleged to appropriate for their owners the bulk of the gains generated by their operations. In order to advance this interest, so it is argued, they exploit their size, their product and market knowledge, their access to financial markets, superior bargaining power and the specific instruments of intra-enterprise pricing. Foreign-dominated multinationals are nevertheless tolerated in many countries precisely because they offer their hosts advantages in the form of technology transfer, managerial know-how, access to markets and other assets represented by ownership advantage.

A review of the conditions which lead to the establishment of bilateral cooperative ventures suggests that the opportunities for this form of bilateral economic cooperation between past belligerents may be rather limited because of the potential for conflict.

On the basis of the above, it is specifically assumed that the host country (B, in the present case) will tolerate the presence of multinationals – that is, foreign-dominated cooperative ventures – only when the foreign party has a clear ownership advantage. This assumption leads to the conclusion that, of the four types of bilateral cooperative ventures, two, namely A_oB_1 and A_1B_o, will be acceptable to the past belligerents. The A_1B_1 variety need not be dominated by either A or B. In fact, there is no *a priori* reason, especially if the output is exported to third countries, why A_1B_1 types of cooperative ventures should be limited to a single enterprise. It may be economically reasonable to establish several plants manufacturing similar products for both domestic and export markets. Some of these plants can be dominated by A and the others by B, as neither has an *a priori* advantage over the other.[12]

A_oB_o type cooperative ventures present more difficult problems, since both inputs have an important component of ownership advantage. The establishment of such ventures is likely to raise more conflicts between A and B than the other types and may, therefore, be avoided or delayed until political and economic relations between the two parties are normalised.

THE ROLE OF THIRD PARTIES

The concept of the cooperative venture can easily be extended to encompass three or more countries. Multi-country cooperative ventures are indispensible when the production process involves more than two inputs and when at least one input per country is required to make the final product internationally competitive.

The variables of the multi-country cooperative ventures are formally specified as follows. Let S_{ji} be the cost of input j in country i (j = 1, ... J; i = 1, ... I). Multi-country cooperative ventures are indispensible when

$$S = \sum_{j=1}^{J} \min_{k=1...I} S_{jk}$$

Each country has at least one input in the production of which it is cheapest; that is, for each i = 1, ... I there exists at least one j_0 such that

$$\min_{k=1...I} S_{j_0 k} = S_{j_0 i}$$

and this is the only case which satisfies

$$S < S_r + t \text{ in the case of import substitution}$$

or

$$S < S_r - t \text{ in the case of export creation}$$

These definitions apply, of course, to any number of countries. To keep the analysis reasonably simple, however, we shall focus herewith on cooperative ventures involving only three countries, A, B and C, where A and B are the recent belligerents and C is a country with which both A and B maintained economic relations in the past. It should be noted that C could be one of many countries and it is therefore perhaps more appropriate to label it as C_i, where i, the specific-country index, can represent a large number of potential candidates.

As with the two-stage production process described above, each stage in the three-stage process of trilateral cooperative ventures is characterised by either ownership or locational advantage. Trilateral cooperative ventures will have one of the eight characteristics listed in Table 4.1.

Thus $A_l B_l C_{il}$ represents a three-stage process where each stage is characterised by location advantage. $A_o B_l C_{il}$ represents a process where A has an ownership advantage, while the inputs contributed by B and C to the cooperative venture are characterised by location advantage. These characteristics have, as already noted, implications regarding the dominance of the cooperative venture. It is assumed, as in the previous case, that all parties dislike foreign dominance, but that they accept foreign domination over the cooperative venture when the foreign party's contribution is characterised by ownership advantage. An additional and essential assumption introduced in the present case is that both A and B prefer domination by C to domination by the other party, especially where C has an ownership advantage.

Indeed, *a priori* reasoning suggests that when C is geographically remote from A and B, its contribution to trilateral cooperative ventures is likely to be

TABLE 4.1

Characteristics of Trilateral Cooperative Ventures

Process characteristics	Dominant party	Nature of dominance
1. $A_1B_0C_{il}$	B	Process characteristics
2. $A_0B_1C_{il}$	A	Process characteristics
3. $A_1B_1C_{io}$	C	Process characteristics
4. $A_1B_0C_{io}$	C	C backed by B
5. $A_0B_1C_{io}$	C	C backed by A
6. $A_0B_0C_{io}$	C	C backed by A and B
7. $A_0B_0C_{il}$	A or B	Conflict
8. $A_1B_1C_{il}$	C?	Arm's-length, conflict or C dominance

characterised more often by ownership than by location advantage. Transfer costs of physical inputs which have little or no component of ownership advantage in them are likely to diminish their competitive edge. Transfer costs are, on the whole, less likely to diminish a competitive advantage when it is derived from proprietary knowledge, management know-how, market information and many of the other factors which constitute ownership advantage.

The possible distribution of the features of trilateral cooperative ventures is shown in Table 4.1, which also describes the process leading to the determination of the party which will tend to dominate the venture in question. Of the eight possibilities, C will be the dominant party in five cases, while A and B will each dominate in one. A conflict over dominance arises in only one case – $A_oB_oC_{il}$, where A and B have an ownership advantage and C_i a location advantage. Even more unpredictable is the case of $A_lB_lC_{il}$.[13] This trilateral cooperative venture, like the bilateral A_lB_l, need not be dominated by any party, since arm's-length transactions are possible and since a natural monopoly is not a necessary feature in those cases where the cooperative venture exports its output to third countries. When the output is marketed in A or B, output of the cooperative venture is likely to be in the declining cost portion of the average cost curve, which implies that no more than a single producer is likely to dominate the market. The cooperative venture will in this case be dominated by the party which possesses the natural monopoly. If the production processes in both A and B have this characteristic, there is likely to be conflict over dominance.

MORE ON THE ROLE OF THIRD PARTIES

Third parties are in a position to make an additional contribution to the economics of peacemaking: their involvement in trilateral cooperative ventures tends to expand the total volume of bilateral transactions between past belligerents. To see why this is so, let us recall the factors which determine the total level of bilateral transactions which A and B are willing to tolerate. If economic welfare considerations alone determined this level, bilateral transactions would be expanded to the point where the marginal transactions level yields zero economic gains. Note, however, that as economic transactions increase, so does A's dependence on B, as an increasing share of A's international transactions is conducted with its recent enemy. What would happen if B were to decide at some point to sever economic relations with A, that is to dissociate? As in export or output creation, cooperative ventures in the case of dissociation imply a loss to A which is larger than the gains from bilateral transactions with B. A must commit resources to support this level of activity. Some of these resources represent fixed investment which can be utilised only in conjunction with bilateral transactions with B – market studies, investments in the design of products which have no alternative markets, investments in plant and equipment intended for export creation, output creation and bilateral cooperative ventures are all examples of outlays which have only limited or no use when economic relations with B are severed.

As was shown in Chapter 2, if B decides to dissociate, A's national income will not revert to the level it would have attained if there had been no bilateral transactions with B in the first place. A's national income will be lower by a larger amount, which is also a function of the level of transactions. Thus both the gains from bilateral transactions and the losses from dissociation rise with the volume of bilateral transactions between the past belligerents. When deciding on the desired level of transactions, the governments of A and B take into consideration the gains from them, the loss due to possible dissociation and the probability of dissociation.

The involvement of third parties in cooperative ventures between A and B affects all three factors. Participation of third parties, in most cases, raises the level of gains. This was amply demonstrated in the last section, which listed the types of cooperative ventures made possible by third-party involvement. By the same token, losses from dissociation are also increased as a result of third-party involvement.

While third-party involvement increases A's losses from dissociation, these losses are not borne by A alone; they are shared with C. Having committed resources to a cooperative venture, C like A (and B) has an economic interest in maintaining the venture as long as revenues exceed marginal costs. This implies that the minimum price required to keep the venture 'in business' is lower (as long as new investments are not required) than the minimum price which the parties expected before they decided to establish the venture in question. Thus, even if B decides to dissociate, C has an economic interest in continuing the venture on a bilateral basis and in sharing with A some losses resulting from B's decision to dissociate.[14]

While C shares these losses with A, there is no *a priori* reason to believe that C's share of the losses is higher than its share of the gains. We return, therefore, to the earlier conclusion, namely that A's gains and losses, given C's involvement, are larger than in the case of C's non-involvement. Third-party involvement will therefore increase expected (rather than unconditional) gains only if its involvement is instrumental in reducing the probability of dissociation. Indeed, this is to be expected, bearing in mind that C's economic interests, given its involvement, are against dissociation. C presumably has some economic and political clout with A and B which it is likely to use in order to safeguard its own economic interests.

In summary, third parties have been shown to make a positive contribution to the economics of peacemaking in two respects: (i) their participation in cooperative ventures increases the range of cooperative transactions between past belligerents which are likely to be economically feasible; (ii) while there are four types of bilateral cooperative ventures, there are eight types of trilateral cooperative ventures. Moreover, since the third party could come from a large number of countries, the absolute number of potentially profitable trilateral cooperative ventures is likely to be much larger than the number of bilateral ones.

Also important is the conflict-reducing element in a third-party presence. A and B are likely, in common with many other countries, to have an aversion for foreign domination of domestic enterprises. Objection to foreign domination when the dominant party is a recent enemy may be stronger still. The presence of third parties from neutral countries is likely to reduce conflict between A and B over domination of trilateral cooperative ventures. In at least five out of the eight hypothetical types of trilateral cooperative ventures listed in Table 4.1, both A and B will probably prefer to let C dominate the cooperative venture, thus reducing the range of conflict without limiting the range of economic cooperation.

Moreover, third-party involvement may be seen by the past belligerents as providing a partial insurance against the other side deciding to dissociate, this also being influenced by possible spill-overs to other transactions of either A or B with the third party. This aspect of third-party involvement combined with its contribution to the increase in unconditional gains will, in many cases, raise expected gains from cooperative ventures and will therefore tend to increase the level of economic transactions between A and B.

CONCLUSIONS

The analysis in Chapters 3 and 4 has a number of implications for the search for goods and services which might be candidates for trade and other kinds of economic transactions between past belligerents.

The instinctive inclination of those interested in identifying areas and candidates for economic cooperation between past belligerents is to start their search by investigating such countries' existing trade. Typically, the researcher interested in, say, A's potential exports to B, examines A's existing exports and B's imports. Those items which are prominent in both countries' trade statistics are identified as potential candidates for bilateral trade. The reasoning behind this tentative conclusion is straightforward. If A exports a good to the rest of the world and if B buys it from the rest of the world, A, which is B's neighbour, ought to have some advantage over those other suppliers who are located further away from B. This reasoning is legitimate, but it has only limited applicability because it focusses on the economically least interesting potential category of goods – trade diversion – and possibly trade expansion. Transactions involving export creation cannot, by definition, be found in A's existing exports. Goods belonging to the output-creation category cannot be found even among A's existing manufacturing industries. These potentially important candidates for transactions between past belligerents must be sought by other, less conventional, methods.[15]

The analysis also yields certain clues regarding the economic and technological characteristics of candidates for bilateral trade between past belligerents. Such candidates are characterised by relatively high transfer costs. Perishables such as fresh fruit, vegetables, meat, milk and milk products come to mind immediately. Cement, quarry products and building materials are other candidates. The list of potential candidates is not exhausted, however, by bulky, low-cost products of the kind mentioned above. Recall that transfer costs also consist of outlays on marketing and provision of services. Proximity to the market can undoubtedly help to reduce service costs of appliances, computer installations, industrial equipment and even the provision of services proper such as medicine, planning, design, insurance and banking. These activities might well figure prominently in the exchange between neighbouring countries.

The production of some candidates for bilateral transactions between recent belligerents is likely to be characterised by economies of scale. Economies of scale on their own are of little importance in the present context. When the manufacture of a product is characterised by negative correlation between volume of output and unit costs, the small size of the domestic market need not prevent the product from being internationally competitive. It is only when transfer costs are substantial that the small size of the domestic market may prove a decisive obstacle. In this case, the opening up of a neighbouring market may be crucial – it may give rise to transactions involving export creation and output creation.

Potential gains from economic intercourse between recent belligerents are not exhausted by trade in goods and services. Further gains are offered by the establishment of cooperative ventures which combine production factors from the two countries and enable the joint enterprises to compete internationally in cases where single-country enterprises are unable to do so. Such ventures may in certain cases compete with imports from third countries. In other cases they may make it possible for the recent belligerents to export jointly to the rest of the world goods and services which they must individually import if they fail to pool their resources.

Cooperative ventures need not be limited to two parties. The addition of third parties increases the list of potentially competitive ventures and total gains from cooperation. It also reduces the risk of dissociation and diminishes the potential conflict over dominance which can inhibit economic cooperation between recent belligerents.

NOTES AND REFERENCES

1. This example assumes constant marginal costs. The analysis and conclusions are unaffected by the type of cost function used.

2. These terms are used widely in the literature on multinational enterprises. For a clear exposition and detailed discussion of these and related terms see John H. Dunning, 'Explaining Changing Patterns of International Production: in Defence of the Eclectic Theory', in Sanjaya Lall (guest editor), *Oxford Bulletin of Economics and Statistics*, Oxford, Special Issue, November 1979.

3. The last statement is not necessarily true for government policies, which may discriminate in favour of or against different categories of enterprises, such as foreign-owned enterprises.

4. For a discussion of the distinction between the characteristics of the goods whose international competitiveness is determined by location advantage, see Hirsch, 'Hypotheses Regarding the Trade Between Developing and Industrialized Countries', in Herbert Giersch (ed.), *The International Division of Labour: Problems and Prospects* (Tübingen: J.C.B. Mohr, for the Institut für Weltwirtschaft an der Universität Kiel, 1974).

5. A formal presentation of the conditions which must be satisfied for international direct investment to take place can be found in Hirsch, 'An International Trade and Investment Theory of the Firm', *op. cit.* See also Dunning, 'Trade, Location of Economic Activity and the Multinational Enterprise: a Search for an Eclectic Approach', in Bertil Ohlin, Per-Ove Hesselborn and Per Magnus Wijkman (eds), *The International Allocation of Economic Activity* (London: Macmillan, 1977), for a detailed exposition using the terminology employed here. For a recent review of the literature on international investment, see Jamuna P. Agarwal, 'Determinants of Foreign Direct Investment: a Survey', *Weltwirtschaftliches Archiv*, Kiel, vol. 116, no. 4, 1980, pp. 739-73.

6. For a discussion of these alternatives to direct foreign investment, see Mark Casson, *Alternatives to the Multinational Enterprise* (London: Macmillan, 1979). See also Peter Buckley and Casson, *The Future of the Multinational Enterprise* (New York: Holmes & Meier, 1979) and Ian Giddy and Alan Rugman, 'A Model of Foreign Direct Investment Trade and Licensing', 1979, mimeograph.

7. Trilateral cooperative ventures are discussed in the following section.

8. For a general equilibrium analysis of vertical integration leading to the establishment of multinational enterprises, see Casson, *op. cit.*, ch. 4.

9. In the case under consideration, such policy may, however, raise objections in country B where the output of the cooperative venture must be marketed.

10. On this point, see, for example, Casson, *op. cit.*; Dunning, 'The Future of the Multinational Enterprise', *Lloyds Bank Review*, London, July 1974; and Hirschman, *How to Divest in Latin America and Why*, Essays in International Finance No. 76 (Princeton: Princeton University Press, 1969).

11. Realisation of the potency of this attitude has led even 'neo-classical' economists such as Albert Breton and Harry G. Johnson to formulate economic theories which treat national ownership of economic enterprises as public goods. See Albert Breton, 'The Economics of Nationalism', *Journal of Political Economy*, August 1964; and Harry G. Johnson, 'A Theoretical Model of Economic Nationalism in New Developing States', *Political Science Quarterly*, Toronto, June 1965.

12. Recall our assumption that $T_{ab} = 0$. If production costs are linear in the sense that $\alpha S = \alpha S_{a1} + \alpha S_{b2} < \alpha(S_r - t)$ (where α is a scalar), it makes no difference whether the assembly of the final product is located in country A or in country B.

13. Recall, however, the statement made earlier that, when C is geographically remote from A

and B, its contribution to trilateral cooperative ventures is likely to have an ownership rather than a location advantage. Cases of the $A_1B_1C_{i1}$ or $A_oB_oC_{i1}$ are likely to be relatively rare.

14. If A decides to dissociate, obviously the same reasoning applies.

15. For examples, see Chapter 5, which discusses methods of projecting trade in different categories between Egypt and Israel.

PART TWO

The Egyptian-Israeli Peace Process

CHAPTER 5

Potential Trade between Egypt and Israel

Trade is the most common mode of international economic transactions. Establishment of trade relations between recent belligerents raises numerous political and economic questions, as was shown in the previous chapters. The present chapter seeks to tackle a seemingly technical problem – developing a methodology for predicting the volume and, more important, the composition of trade between recent belligerents, that is, neighbouring countries which have not traded with each other in the recent past. The methodology, which uses some of the concepts developed in Chapter 3, is demonstrated on Egyptian-Israeli trade.

For a long time to come the volume and composition of trade and other economic transactions between Egypt and Israel will undoubtedly be influenced to an important degree by political considerations. It is inconceivable that in the foreseeable future the two governments will allow economic and other transactions between their citizens to be determined solely by economic considerations. Progress in the negotiations concerning the establishment of an Autonomy in the West Bank and Gaza regions, as provided for in the Egyptian-Israeli Peace Treaty, intra-Arab relations, East-West and North-South relations as well as domestic political, social and economic developments will all affect the readiness of the two governments to allow and encourage economic intercourse between their citizens.

In spite of the centrality of the political considerations, it is important to look at the potential for trade and other transactions between the countries from a purely economic point of view, especially since this potential is not a given quantity, waiting to be discovered and exploited like a natural resource or a physical entity. It is determined by numerous factors, some of which may, in turn, be subject to influence by policy decisions. The realisation of this potential will require planning, allocation of resources and time. Consequently, it makes sense to try to estimate the volume and composition of potential trade and other transactions between Egypt and Israel, regardless of the uncertainties about political conditions and the institutional framework of these transactions, even though these factors will surely have a profound influence on the realisation of the estimates.

In Chapter 3 we outlined the characteristics of different types of transactions – export diversion, export and import expansion, export and output creation. Short-term trade projections made by various government institutions in Israel point to a modest potential which accounts for no more than 1 or 2 per cent of Israel's total international trade. These projections, by their very nature, pertain mainly to trade diversion; that is, to the displacement of existing trade with other markets by trade between Egypt and Israel. This type of estimate has relevance to the short term when production patterns cannot be changed. When examining longer-term trade potential – that is, when production capacity can be changed – other elements have to be taken into consideration, particularly special advantages of trade between neighbouring countries.[1]

The theoretical analysis in Chapter 3 showed that the export- and import-diversion categories need not represent a major proportion of total potential trade between recent belligerents – that is, between countries about to establish trade relations *de novo*. The other categories, namely trade expansion, export creation and output creation, can be very important. Seeking to identify products belonging to these groups, we must examine the experience of other countries which do trade bilaterally.

In the following analysis we combine all the above categories under the heading of trade expansion and introduce an additional category – trade diversion (which should not be confused with this term as it is applied to integration theory). The first group includes those products whose tradeability is hampered by high transfer costs and which are, consequently, unlikely to figure prominently in Egypt's or Israel's current trade, since most of the former's and all of the latter's international trade is conducted with overseas countries. Trade diversion pertains to all cases where existing trade between Israel and Egypt with the rest of the world is likely to be displaced by trade between them, regardless of welfare gains.

Two approaches to identifying goods with these characteristics are examined in this chapter. The first, which is rather simple and straightforward, utilises the notion of border trade. It is discussed in the next section. The second approach is based on the assumption that transfer costs change systematically with distance. To the extent that this assumption is realistic, trade between pairs of countries will, *ceteris paribus*, be smaller, the larger the physical distance between them. This approach is discussed in the following section. In the final section, the results are applied to Israeli and Egyptian trade data. This section also contains an analysis of the potential for trade diversion between the two countries.

BORDER TRADE

Border trade, as the term suggests, concerns the exchange of goods and services between neighbouring countries. In the neo-classical world, where transfer costs do not exist, border trade is of no particular interest. In a world where transfer costs are positive and increase as a function of distance, border trade can be viewed as a limiting case of international trade. In those cases where transfer charges account for a very high proportion of delivered costs, international trade is limited to countries with common borders.[2] Goods traded only between neighbouring countries should properly be regarded as non-tradeables, since there is no logical reason why (abstracting from administrative restrictions) goods and services which must be sold in close proximity to where they are being produced cannot be sold just across the border, when the border is close.

Border trade in the present context is viewed from a somewhat different angle. Our concern is not with goods which are only traded between neighbours, but with goods mainly traded between neighbours. Accordingly, products are regarded as belonging to the border-trade category if a high proportion of trade in them is between neighbouring countries. Products thus identified are obviously *prima facie* candidates for trade between Egypt and Israel.

The trade data of Egypt and Israel do not lend themselves to the kind of analysis suggested above. Since Israel's neighbours do not trade with her, Israel has no border trade. Egypt's trade with her neighbours, Sudan and Libya, is very limited owing to geographic and other considerations. It was therefore necessary to establish the list of potential border-trade goods on the basis of the experience of other countries. The actual analysis was performed on data pertaining to three small European countries: the Netherlands, Switzerland and Ireland. Of the three, Switzerland is landlocked, her neighbours being West Germany, France, Austria and Italy. The Netherlands borders on two large countries, West Germany and France, as well as the much smaller Belgium. The Republic of Ireland has common borders only with the province of Northern Ireland, which is part of the United Kingdom, Ireland's closest trading partner.

Before discussing the results, we ought briefly to consider the data. Published trade statistics pertain to bundles of goods which are grouped arbitrarily under a single heading or statistical category. The goods listed in a specific category may or may not conform to our notion of homogeneous products. Products contained in a single category may have high transfer costs and others belonging to the same classification may have very low transfer costs. The problem of aggregation which this type of analysis always presents is not new and there are no obvious ways of overcoming it. If we were doing actual market research, we would have used more disaggregated data. Since the purpose of this particular exercise is to demonstrate a method, 2-digit and

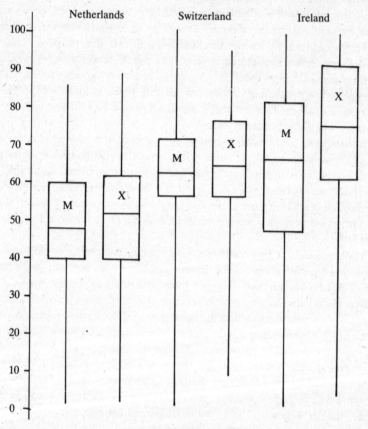

FIGURE 5.1
Box Plots of Border-trade Figures·

3-digit groups in the Standard International Trade Classification (SITC) were used. This broad classification may well bias some results by obscuring some relevant characteristic of sub-groups and individual products. These points should be taken into account when interpreting the results.

The distribution of border-trade figures of various industries in the three countries in 1978 is depicted in Figure 5.1 by means of box plots. Each box describes border exports or imports of the country in question as a percentage of total trade. Boxes consist of three lines: the upper and lower lines capture between them 50 per cent of the country's border trade; the top line shows the upper and the bottom line the lower quartiles of either border exports or imports. The median percentage of border trade is shown by the middle line. The box plot on the left, for example, pertains to the Netherlands' border imports. Figure 5.1 displays the following information:

(a) Border imports ranged between a high of 84 per cent and a low of 2 per cent of total trade.

(b) In the lowest quartile (25 per cent of the value of border imports), border trade accounted for less than 41 per cent of total trade.

(c) In the highest quartile, border trade accounted for more than 61 per cent of total trade.

(d) The median was 49 per cent – that is, half the border trade was less than 49 per cent – while the border trade of the other half exceeded 49 per cent. The dotted lines continue beyond the upper and lower quartiles to the extreme values.

As expected, variations in border-trade percentages are very large, ranging from 100 per cent in the case of gas or mineral tar and crude chemicals from coal in Ireland's exports to 2 per cent in nuts and kernels in the Netherlands' imports. The distribution of the middle 50 per cent, however, is concentrated between 45 per cent (the Netherlands' lowest quartile of border exports and imports) and 92 per cent (Ireland's highest quartile of border exports).

Variations among countries and between imports and exports are to be expected. They can be explained by product characteristics, such as perishability and dependence on services, availability of natural resources or other natural conditions, such as climate, type of soil and access to ports, and other cost factors, such as value in relation to weight. Thus it is hardly surprising that tobacco and most metals do not figure prominently in the border trade of Switzerland, the Netherlands and Ireland or that gas accounts for a high proportion of border trade in some countries but not in others.

The border-trade data comprise a total of six categories, denoted by $j = 1 \ldots 6$ (exports and imports for three countries). Each category naturally displays somewhat different characteristics from the point of view of the industry's affinity to border trade. To facilitate the analysis it was necessary to represent the industries' characteristics by means of a single normalised measure. For each industry a normalised border-trade index was computed.

Normalisation consists of the following steps:

(1)   For each industry and each category, compute B_{ij}, the percentage share of border trade in total trade:

$$B_{ij} = \frac{\cdot \; \text{border trade of i}}{\text{total trade of i}}$$

where

i is the industry index, $i = 1 \dots 58$
j is the category index, $j = 1 \dots 6$

(2)   For each category, compute average border trade B_j:

$$B_j = \frac{\text{total border trade}}{\text{total trade}}$$

Also compute variance of border trade:

$$VAR_j = \sum_{i=1}^{I} B^2_{ij} \; \text{trade i/total trade} - B^2_j$$

(3)   Normalised border-trade indices, NB_{ij}, are obtained by deducting B_j from the original figure and dividing by the standard deviation of B_{ij}:

$$NB_{ij} = (B_{ij} - B_j) / \sqrt{VAR_j}$$

(4)   The average normalised border-trade index for each industry, NB_i, is finally arrived at by computing the average of NB_{ij} over all values of j:

$$NB_i = \sum_{j=1}^{6} NB_{ij} / 6$$

A positive index indicates that the industry's border trade was on average higher than the total border trade. Industries with positive indices are considered to be candidates for trade expansion and trade creation. Their eligibility for trade between neighbouring countries is assumed to vary positively with the value of the index.

Table 5.1 lists the ten industries with the highest and the ten with the lowest border-trade indices. The upper part of the table shows products which are mostly consumed or used in the neighbourhood of where they are produced. Gas and live animals, which belong to this list, can and in fact are being transported over long distances when necessary. A high proportion of trade appears, however, to be limited to short distances because of high transport costs.

TABLE 5.1

Industries with the Highest and Lowest Border-trade Indices

SITC	Industry	Border-trade index
HIGH		
96	Coins (not legal tender)	2.45
34	Gas, natural and manufactured	2.02
00	Live animals	1.82
82	Furniture	1.75
81	Sanitary, plumbing, heating and lighting fixtures	1.70
41	Animal oils and fats	1.48
57	Explosives and pyrotechnic products	1.33
84	Clothing	1.30
43	Animal and vegetable oils and fats, processed, and waxes	1.18
24	Wood, lumber, cork	1.18
LOW		
12	Tobacco	−1.62
91	Postal packages not classified	−0.96
07	Coffee, cocoa, tea, spices	−0.77
86	Scientific, medical, optical, photographic and precision instruments	−0.66
59	Chemical products and materials n.e.s.	−0.47
93	Special transactions not classified according to kind	−0.46
11	Beverages	−0.34
51	Chemicals	−0.29
54	Medicinal and pharmaceutical products	−0.25
42	Vegetable-oil products	−0.17

The bottom part of the table contains typical foot-loose goods. Some of these, like coffee, tea and tobacco, are agricultural products which depend on specific climatic conditions. Traditionally, they have occupied a prominent place in international trade. Other products in this group, such as precision instruments and medicinal and pharmaceutical products, which are high-technology goods, are manufactured by a relatively small number of firms possessing specialised knowledge and experience. Their unit value is typically high and they figure prominently in international trade, mostly in the exports of the highly industrialised countries.

The implications of these findings for Egyptian-Israeli border trade are considered in a subsequent section, where they are combined with the empirical results of another trade-predicting model.

A LINEAR REGRESSION MODEL

This section describes a more general model of trade, which relates trade explicitly to several factors, including those pertaining to border trade. The model employed here is similar in many respects to the model used by Hans Linnemann, of the Institute of Social Studies at The Hague, in his study of the elements influencing the overall network of world trade.[3]

In his study Professor Linnemann used three categories of explanatory variables:

   (a) factors indicating total potential supply of the exporting country to the world market;

   (b) factors indicating total potential demand of the importing country from the world market; and

   (c) factors representing 'resistance' to trade flows from the potential supplier to the potential buyer.

In Professor Linnemann's study, total potential demand for imports and total potential supply of exports were represented by the gross national product (GNP) of the importing and exporting countries, respectively. Since our concern is with individual industries and not merely with aggregate trade, it was necessary to construct a more elaborate model than Professor Linne-mann's. Accordingly, overall demand for, and supply of, specific industries are represented both by GNP of the importing and exporting countries and by total imports and exports of the industries under consideration.

Following Professor Linnemann, we use geographic distance between trading partners to represent trade resistance. Distance is in this case a proxy for transfer costs. Other things being equal, the greater the transfer costs between two countries, the smaller is the trade flow. The relative magnitude of transfer costs, however, varies with different commodities. The cost of shipping an article from one country to another depends on a number of considerations: weight, bulk, value, physical characteristics, the distance traversed, the mode and speed of transportation, the character of the route, existence of other cargoes shipped between the same points, especially in the opposite direction, and so on.[4] Geographic distance is used as a measure of trade resistance between two countries, even though transfer costs per unit of distance, for any given product, are not necessarily the same everywhere (the differences, being due mainly to geographic factors, are assumed to be minor and negligible).

Other things being equal, it is assumed that the larger the importance of the distance factor, the more advantageous will be trade between neighbouring countries.

A different variable representing resistance to trade is 'economic distance', measured here by the difference between the per capita incomes of the trading partners. This measure represents the sum of two different factors. The first, based on the Burenstam Linder model of trade determination, stresses the costs of adjusting domestic products to suit the specifications of foreign markets.[5] Assuming that countries with similar per capita income have similar tastes, Professor Burenstam Linder asserts that countries with similar per capita income will trade with each other more intensively than countries with diverging incomes. Adjustment costs naturally vary between countries, thus giving varying weights to economic distance.

The second factor also represented by economic distance is the degree of comparative advantage in production of the exporting country. This follows from the Heckscher-Ohlin model relating comparative costs to relative endowments, which can easily be related to per capita incomes. Contrary to the Burenstam Linder factor, the larger the economic distance, the higher is the comparative advantage and the stronger are the incentives to trade. The measure of economic distance used in this model makes it possible to estimate only the sum of the above two effects.[6] In cases where the Burenstam Linder effect predominates, economic distance will have a negative sign and where the Heckscher-Ohlin effect predominates, economic distance will have a positive sign. When the two effects cancel each other out, economic distance will be indeterminate.

Unlike geographic distance, which is small in the case of Israel and Egypt, economic distance is large. Therefore, *ceteris paribus,* the lower the sensitivity to the Burenstam Linder effect and the higher the sensitivity to the Heckscher-Ohlin effect, the larger is the potential for trade expansion.

For every product, h, a function is fitted which relates bilateral trade figures over all pairs of countries to the following variables:

(a) potential supply of the exporting country, as measured by its total exports of the product and by its GNP;

(b) potential demand of the importing country, as measured by total imports of the product from all countries and by the GNP of the importing country; and

(c) geographic and economic distances between the trading partners – variables measuring resistance to trade.

The model includes the following elements:

$$M_h(i,j) = f[GNP(j), GNP(i), DGNP(i,j), DIST(i,j), TM_h(j), TX_h(i)]$$

where

$M_h(i,j)$	=	imports of product h by country j from country i
i	=	index of exporting country
j	=	index of importing country
h	=	product index
GNP(i)	=	GNP of exporting country
$TX_h(i)$	=	total exports of product h by exporting country
GNP(j)	=	GNP of importing country
$TM_h(j)$	=	total imports of product h by importing country

The last two variables are:

DIST(i,j)	=	geographic distance between exporting and importing countries
DGNP(i,j)	=	absolute value of difference between per capita incomes of importing and exporting countries (measures the economic distance between the two countries)

A multiplicative regression equation was used to estimate the effects of the above factors in different products with a view to comparing the varying effects of the factors in (c) among the products. The regression equation estimated for each product, h, has the form:

$$\log[M_h(i,j)] = A_h + B_h\log[GNP(i)] + C_h\log[GNP(j)] \\ + D_h\log[TX_h(i)] + E_h\log[TM_h(j)] \\ + F_h\log[DIST(i,j)] + G_h\log[DGNP(i,j)]$$

The coefficients B_h to E_h are expected to be positive for every h (both supply and demand of the exporting and importing countries, respectively, are positively correlated with their GNPs and total exports and imports of that product). F_h is expected to be negative (trade declines with distance). The coefficient of G_h can be either positive or negative, depending on whether the Burenstam Linder effect overwhelms the Heckscher-Ohlin effect or *vice versa*.

Regression models of the kind shown here can in principle be used to estimate the volume of bilateral trade between pairs of countries. Estimates of trade flows in either direction between, say, Egypt and Israel can be obtained by plugging in the appropriate country and industry data. At this stage, however, we do not have sufficient confidence in the model and in the data at our disposal to justify this kind of exercise. We make use of the model to accomplish a more modest objective – to identify those industries which are likely candidates for trade between two neighbouring countries. Identification of industry characteristics is in this case based on a large number of observations and, in most cases, the sampling error is small enough to justify the observations and conclusions reported in the following pages.

RESULTS OF THE REGRESSION MODEL

Lack of data on world trade flows obliged us to use trade figures of the Organisation for Economic Cooperation and Development (OECD) for the analysis. The data used cover trade within OECD countries and between OECD countries and the rest of the world.[7] The figures do not include trade between non-OECD countries. Since OECD trade accounts for a high proportion of world trade, the distortion caused by missing trade figures is unlikely to be too serious, especially if we bear in mind that the purpose of the analysis is not to predict levels of trade flows but only to identify product groups which are sensitive to physical and economic distance.

The data at our disposal made it possible to construct equations covering 58 product groups, using once again the 2-digit and 3-digit SITC classification. The regression coefficients were obtained by a step-wise procedure in which non-significant variables were omitted. (As a rule of thumb, all variables with F values less than 2.5 were excluded. About 250 observations were available for each regression estimation.) The detailed results of the regression calculations are presented in the tables which comprise Appendix 2. In this section we confine ourselves to outlining the summaries of the results, relating to Professor Linnemann's three categories of explanatory variables described above.

Demand

Demand, as was noted earlier, is represented by two parameters: the GNP of the importing country and $TM_h(j)$, total imports of that product by the importing country. The following histograms ('stem and leaf displays') present the values of coefficients estimated.

In this and in the following displays the stems (the numbers on the far left) should be added to the leaves to form the exact distribution of values. In

DISPLAY 1
Coefficient of GNP(j) – C_h

0.0	
0.1	9 2 8 6 5 2 7 9
0.2	3 4 4 0 6 9 7 6 7
0.3	5 7 9 1 3 0 8 0 9 4 3 6 3 7 0
0.4	8 5 1 7 6 5
0.5	0 1 2 7 2
0.6	7
0.7	
0.8	

DISPLAY 2
Coefficient of $TM_h(j)$ – E_h

0.2	9
0.3	6 2
0.4	
0.5	8 1 7 9
0.6	8 3 3 1 6
0.7	2 2 3 8 7 1 1 1 4 2 3
0.8	6 7 6 6 8 9 8 7 9 1 3 9 3
0.9	3 7 2 3 6 0 7 3 2
1.0	0 6 2 3 3 7
1.1	0 7 8
1.2	4
1.3	3
1.4	6 5 9

Display 1, for example, the numbers in the first row should read: 0.19, 0.12, 0.18, 0.16, 0.15, 0.12, 0.17 and 0.19, while that on the 0.6 stem is 0.67.

DISPLAY 3
Coefficient of GNP(i) – B_h

0.0	
0.1	5 9 7 4
0.2	5 4 7 9 6 5 1 5 2 9
0.3	8 8 3 0 1 3 4 2 5 6
0.4	0 3 3 4 0 7 7
0.5	2 2 8 3 1
0.6	9 2 5 0

DISPLAY 4
Coefficient of $TX_h(i)$ – D_h

0.4	7 2 8
0.5	8
0.6	3 7 8
0.7	1 8 9 5 4 6 8 6
0.8	0 6 5 6 7 7 5 9
0.9	8 7 2 7 7 8 4
1.0	6 4 8 2 5 5 9 0 7 2 3 0
1.1	2 6 0 0 6 7 2
1.2	8 5 0 0
1.3	9 5 4
1.4	2
1.5	
1.6	4 9

Supply

In an analogous way supply is represented by the GNP of the exporting country and total exports by the exporting country of that product. The values of the coefficients obtained are presented in Displays 3 and 4. As anticipated all coefficients are positive.

Values of $TM_h(j)$, denoting industry effects, tend to be higher than values of $GNP(i)$, denoting country effects. This suggests that demand for imports is more sensitive to industry-specific than to country-specific factors. The same pattern is repeated by the $TX_h(i)$ and $GNP(i)$ coefficients. In the case of exports, too, industry-specific factors appear to influence trade flows more strongly than country-specific factors.

Comparison between the $GNP(i)$ and $GNP(j)$ coefficients indicates that exporting-country and importing-country effects tend to be distributed similarly. Note, for example, that the values tend to be bounded from below by 0.1 and above by 0.6 in both cases. The distribution of $TM_h(j)$ and $TX_h(i)$ is characterised by more variations. Note the wider dispersion of $TM_h(j)$ and,

DISPLAY 5

Coefficient of $DIST(i,j) - F_h$

−0.9	0 7
−0.8	9 5 4
−0.7	6 2 0 4
−0.6	4 8 5 4 0 4 7 5 9 7 3 6 2 0 4 9 3
−0.5	4 0 2 3 7 3 2 0 0 7 9 8 1 8 4 6 3 3
−0.4	9 8 8 8 8 1
−0.3	8 9 2 2
−0.2	3 7 0
−0.1	
−0.0	

more importantly, the higher values of $TX_h(i)$. Note also that the median of the $TX_h(i)$ coefficient, which denotes elasticity of the industry's supply, is unity, whereas the median of the $TM_h(j)$ coefficient is less than unity (0.86). Industry-specific factors of the exporters tend to influence trade flows more than industry-specific factors in the importing country.

Resistance Parameters

Two variables are used to measure resistance to trade: the first and more important – geographic distance – is denoted by $DIST(i,j)$. Its coefficient, F_h, is, as expected, significantly different from zero in all but one regression equation and all the coefficients are negative. Elasticity of the distance factor tends to be relatively high, exceeding 0.5 in most cases. This means that for the typical product an increase in distance of 10 per cent will reduce trade by between 5 and 6 per cent. Distance is clearly a factor which retards trade in many products.

The second variable measuring resistance to trade is the difference of per capita GNP of the exporting and importing countries. As explained earlier, this factor has two opposite effects. Consequently, in many regression equations the value of the coefficient is not significantly different from zero, as the two opposite effects cancel each other out. The following stem and leaf display presents only those coefficients found to be significantly different from zero.

DISPLAY 6
Coefficient of $DGNP(i,j) - G_h$

−0.5	
−0.4	
−0.3	7 0
−0.2	0 2
−0.1	7 1 5 7 6
−0.0	8
0.0	9
0.1	5 6 4
0.2	0 6
0.3	1
0.4	0
0.5	

In order to simplify the analysis, a combined measure of resistance to trade taking into account the effects of $DGNP(i,j)$ and $DIST(i,j)$ was devised:

$$RES_h(i,j) = F_h + G_h \frac{\log 1050 - \log 3420}{\log 2000 - \log 300}$$

This measure compares both distance and per capita income differences between Israel and Egypt with those between Israel and her alternative destination of trade – the European Community. The numerator measures the difference of GNP per capita differences between Israel and the European Community ($1,050) and between Israel and Egypt ($3,420) and the denominator the difference of distances from Israel to the European Community (2,000 km) and from Israel to Egypt (300 km). $RES_h(i,j)$ is constructed such that it needs computing only when G_h is significantly different from zero. Otherwise, it equals F_h. Its values are presented in the

DISPLAY 7
Weighted coefficient of DGNP(i,j) and DIST(i,j):$RES_h(i,j)$

−1.0	1
−0.9	0
−0.8	1 3 5 8 9
−0.7	0 2 5 6 8
−0.6	0 0 3 4 4 4 4 4 5 7 7 8 9 9
−0.5	0 0 1 2 2 3 3 3 4 5 6 7 7 8 8 9
−0.4	8 8 8 8 9
−0.3	1 9 9 9
−0.1	2 3 8
−0.0	
0.0	0

DISPLAY 8
R^2

0.1	
0.2	
0.3	9 5 9 2.1 7
0.4	1 8 8 4 9
0.5	9 9 5 6 4 7 5 0 2 1 0 8
0.6	3 6 9 8 7 1
0.7	3 2 4 5 5 2 1 8 1 9 7 6 1 7 8 9 0 4 2 3 2 4
0.8	2 2 6 6 1 4
0.9	0

last column of Table A.4 in Appendix 2. A stem and leaf display of their values is shown in Display 7.

The distribution of $RES_h(i,j)$ is quite similar to that of DIST(i,j), indicating the importance of physical in relation to economic distance. This is hardly surprising in view of the fact that the separate factors determining economic distance cancel each other out, as we have seen.

The regression equations used account for (on average) 70 per cent of the variations of the dependent variable. Display 8 depicts the value of the coefficients of determination of the regressions of trade in the various industries.

Table 5.2 lists five product groups with the highest and with the lowest sensitivity to distance (the full list of industries is presented in Table A.2 of Appendix 2). The top of the table shows products that are highly sensitive to physical and economic distance. The criteria for inclusion were either a high (negative) distance coefficient or a high (negative) weighted coefficient. The lower part of the table shows products whose tradeability is positively correlated with physical distance and with the combined distance index.

It is not surprising that the two sections have several common products, such as live animals, gas, furniture or sanitary, plumbing, heating and lighting fixtures, which are sensitive to distance and have high percentages of border trade, and precision instruments, tobacco, medicinal and pharmaceutical products and chemicals on the side with low sensitivity to distance and low border-trade indices. After all, if a product is highly sensitive to distance, it is likely, *ceteris paribus,* to figure more prominently in trade conducted between neighbours than between more distant trading partners.

Having grouped the different products on the basis of their sensitivity to distance, let us examine the usefulness of this approach to the identification of candidates for bilateral trade between Egypt and Israel.

POTENTIAL EGYPTIAN-ISRAELI TRADE PATTERNS

Chapter 3 specified different categories of transactions between neighbouring countries, including export diversion, import and export expansion and export and output creation. The distinction between the different categories was shown to be strongly influenced by their sensitivity to transfer costs and economies of scale. We have no direct evidence about the effect of transfer costs on different products traded internationally. In the previous section, however, we presented some evidence about the sensitivity to distance of different product groups. If we accept the hypothesis that products which are sensitive to distance (in the sense that their tradeability is negatively correlated with distance) are characterised by a higher ratio of transfer to total costs, we are justified in applying the findings reported in the last two sections to the prediction of trading patterns between Egypt and Israel.

TABLE 5.2
Highest and Lowest Resistance to Trade Parameters

SITC	Industry	Coefficient of DIST(i,j) F_h	Combined coefficient $RES_h(i,j)$
HIGH TRADE RESISTANCE			
91	Postal packages not classified according to kind	−0.97	−0.78
81	Sanitary, plumbing, heating and lighting fixtures	−0.91	−0.91
00	Live animals	−0.90	−0.90
03	Fish	−0.85	−0.85
33	Petroleum and petroleum products	−0.80	−1.01
34	Gas, natural and manufactured	−0.76	−0.76
84	Clothing and accessories	−0.74	−0.83
67	Iron and steel	−0.73	−0.30
68	Non-ferrous metals	−0.70	−0.70
821	Furniture	−0.69	−0.69
55	Essential oils, perfume materials, toilet and cleansing goods	−0.69	−0.69
LOW TRADE RESISTANCE			
86	Scientific, medical, optical photographic, and precision instruments	−0.41	−0.31
41	Animal oils and fats	−0.39	−0.39
02	Milk and egg products	−0.38	−0.25
51	Chemicals	−0.33	−0.19
42	Vegetable oils	−0.33	−0.13
22	Oil seeds, oil nuts and oil kernels	−0.28	−0.28
21	Hides and skins	−0.23	0
54	Medicinal and pharmaceutical products	−0.21	−0.14
12	Tobacco	0	0

The category considered first is export diversion. The technique used here to identify export-diversion candidates does not depend on the results of the regression or border-trade analysis. It is suggested by the straightforward interpretation of the term 'diversion', which implies the shifting of existing exports from one market to another, or, in the case under consideration, displacing existing trade between Egypt and Israel with other markets by bilateral trade.

To start with, let us recall that this option is not necessarily economically advantageous to either side. For example, if Israel diverts exports from Europe to Egypt in such a way that the f.o.b. prices which Israel charges Egypt are the same as those she charges a European country, and these equal the c.i.f. prices Egypt had previously paid for the same product, then both Israel and Egypt are essentially indifferent to the possibilities of trading with each other. Trade diversion where nobody gains is unlikely to take place in reality, since neither seller nor buyer has an economic interest in such transactions. It is possible, on the other hand, that even modest transfer-cost savings will result in substantial trade diversion between two neighbouring countries.

A product is considered here to have a trade-diversion potential when one country is a net exporter of that product, whereas the other is a net importer; or, in formal notation, country A is said to have a potential for trade diversion in product j *vis-à-vis* country B when

$$NX_{aj} = X_{aj} - M_{aj} > 0$$

and

$$NX_{bj} = X_{bj} - M_{bj} < 0$$

where
  X_{ij} = exports of country i of product j
  M_{ij} = imports of country i of product j

The maximum potential diversion (only part of which may actually be realised) will then be the smaller of the net exports and net imports of the two countries or

$$\text{Maximum trade diversion} = \text{Minimum } \{NX_{aj} - NX_{bj}\}$$

This definition is rather conservative and may appear to be overly restrictive.

Conceptually, the term diversion pertains to the actual output of an industry. At any given moment, output (assuming that available capacity is fully utilised) is divided between domestic and export sales. Increased demand made possible by the removal of trade barriers can be catered for in the short run by diverting supplies from either the domestic market or third countries. The present definition of diversion potential is based on the assumption that transfer costs, consisting of international transportation and handling charges, as well as the excess of export over domestic marketing costs, are positive.[8] *Ceteris paribus*, a supplier will not, therefore, divert domestic sales to export markets. It is further assumed that exports to a new market, especially a market which was hitherto completely inaccessible, are viewed as risky and requiring substantial investments in market research, the establishment of outlets and other mechanisms to facilitate market penetration. In the short run, these outlays may well outweigh the cost savings due to the shorter distances. Consequently, only firms with a strong export performance will consider diverting exports from existing markets to that of the recent enemy. An industry with a positive trade balance is here regarded as having demonstrated a strong export performance.

Similar reasoning applies to the importing country. Importing from a new supplier is assumed to be a viable proposition in the short run, only if the country has demonstrated competitive disadvantage with regard to the product under consideration. A negative trade balance is here considered a sufficient demonstration of such a disadvantage.

The approach outlined above was applied to the trade data of Egypt for 1977 and Israel for 1978.[9] Industries were paired on the basis of 2-digit and 3-digit SITC classification. They were divided into three groups, representing different trade expansion potential, on the basis of the information obtained from the regression and border-trade analysis discussed in the last section. The grouping was based on the values of the regression coefficients of resistance to trade $[RES_h(i,j)]$ and distance (F_h) and of the border-trade indices. Industries whose regression coefficients were in the lowest quartile were assigned to the high expansion-potential group.[10] Industries whose regression coefficients were in the inter-quartile range – that is, which were larger than the lower quartile and smaller than the upper quartile – and those whose border-trade averages were above the average are included in the ordinary trade expansion-potential group. The remaining industries – that is, those with very high regression coefficients (in the upper quartile) or with low border-trade indices – were considered to have little trade-expansion potential. The results are shown in Table 5.3.

Table 5.4 lists industries with a more promising expansion potential. These

TABLE 5.3
Diversion Potential
(thousand US$)

SITC	Industry	Israeli exports 1978	Israeli imports 1978	Egyptian exports 1977	Egyptian imports 1977	Diversion potential[a]
A	ISRAEL TO EGYPT ONLY					
59	Chemical materials and products n.e.s.	112,543	59,134	408	92,907	53,409
513-5	Inorganic chemicals	63,939	42,947	31	41,040	20,992
42	Vegetable oil	8,710	7,758	28	11,768	952
Sub-total A		185,192	109,839	467	145,715	75,353

[a] Defined as the minimum between the exporting country's net exports and the importing country's net imports.

TABLE 5.4
Diversion and Expansion Potential
(thousand US$)

SITC	Industry	Israeli exports 1978	Israeli imports 1978	Egyptian exports 1977	Egyptian imports 1977	Diversion potential[a]
B	EGYPT TO ISRAEL					
33[bd]	Petroleum and petroleum products	302	774,697	413,461	28,166	385,295
65[bd]	Textile yarn, fabrics and made-up goods	80,584	128,739	268,888	76,516	48,155
684[bd]	Aluminium	19,196	64,913	32,047	6,011	26,036
042[c]	Rice	0	11,971	59,744	0	11,971
55[bd]	Essential oils, perfume materials, toilet and cleansing goods	5,527	16,870	48,872	20,386	11,343
075[b]	Spices	65	2,876	10,829	2,280	2,811
85[d]	Footwear	4,511	6,825	13,425	464	2,314
666[bd]	Pottery	398	2,677	36	3,490	2,279
82[bd]	Furniture	12,947	17,710	6,748	4,782	1,966
611,613[d]	Leather; fur skins	5,872	19,571	1,774	424	1,350
265,267[d]	Vegetable fibres, except cotton and jute; waste materials from textile fabrics	38	1,086	10,685	1,160	1,048
83[d]	Travel goods, handbags et cetera	499	1,757	2,655	1,659	996
291	Crude animal materials n.e.s.	306	913	1,221	126	607
045[c]	Cereals, unmilled, excluding wheat, rice, barley and maize	122	72,799	343	0	343
57[bd]	Explosives and pyrotechnic products	272	585	670	138	313
	Sub-total B	130,669	1,123,989	871,401	145,602	496,827

SITC	Industry	Israeli exports 1978	Israeli imports 1978	Egyptian exports 1977	Egyptian imports 1977	Diversion potential[a]
C	ISRAEL TO EGYPT					
69[d]	Manufactures of metal	387,712	94,024	3,347	220,094	216,747
56[c]	Manufactured fertilisers	89,027	1,868	625	39,066	38,441
89[d]	Miscellaneous manufactures n.e.s.	127,089	94,853	21,239	70,705	32,326
62[d]	Rubber manufactures	41,955	17,985	228	41,986	23,970
734-5	Aircraft, ships and boats	152,725	135,190	9	43,168	17,535
012,013	Meat, dried, salted or smoked; meat in airtight containers n.e.s. and meat preparations	7,799	5	4	7,359	7,355
02[c]	Milk and milk products	12,566	8,083	64	66,811	4,483
08[c]	Feedstuff for animals	10,634	7,600	2,758	23,972	3,034
726	Electrical apparatus for medical and radiological use	11,437	8,420	0	3,423	3,017
284[b]	Non-ferrous metal scrap	3,558	701	39	3,236	2,857
09[d]	Margarine and shortening; food preparations n.e.s.	9,918	4,193	3,718	6,337	2,619
048	Cereal preparations	2,617	1,991	952	3,952	626
073[b]	Chocolate and other food preparations containing cocoa	2,315	797	21	224	203
292	Crude vegetable materials n.e.s.	90,223	12,557	13,098	13,018	80
842[bd]	Fur clothing and articles of fur	9,743	272	0	13	13
667[bd]	Pearls, precious and semi-precious stones	1,499,740	1,344,831	0	1	1
	Sub-total C	2,489,058	1,733,370	43,622	543,365	353,307

[a] Defined as the minimum between the exporting country's net exports and the importing country's net imports.
[b] Extremely profitable expansion-wise; that is, in the lower 2.5 per cent of industries ranked by their distance coefficient or by combined resistance coefficient.
[c] Implied only from border-trade calculations.
[d] Implied both from relevant regression coefficients and border-trade calculations.

TABLE 5.5

High Expansion Potential

(thousand US$)

SITC	Industry	Israeli exports 1978	Israeli imports 1978	Egyptian exports 1977	Egyptian imports 1977	Product category[a]
64[b]	Paper, paperboard and manufactured products	4,078	83,655	359	114,211	B
67[b]	Iron and steel	11,344	272,683	4,781	175,571	B
06[b]	Sugar, honey and products	2,168	47,402	29,416	43,169	B
81[b]	Sanitary, plumbing, heating and lighting fixtures	391	6,867	175	7,517	B
28 excluding 284	Iron, steel, silver, platinum, uranium and thorium ores, scrap and concentrates	732	54,712	0	12,086	B
00[b]	Live animals	6,632	812	4,687	4,361	A
91	Postal packages not classified according to kind	2,400	52	0	0	C
34[b]	Gas, natural and manufactured	0	579	0	10,337	B
07 excluding 073,075	Coffee, cocoa and tea	426	69,268	0	85,150	B
84[b] excluding 842	Clothing, excluding fur clothing	146,855	18,119	38,658	15,328	A
66[b] excluding 666,667	Lime, cement, fabricated building material, clay, construction material, mineral manufactures, glass and glassware	14,855	56,218	2,098	119,549	B
68[b] excluding 684	Non-ferrous metals, except for aluminium	5,701	81,555	0	21,397	B
03[b]	Fish	3,063	15,325	6,103	24,819	B
731-3	Transport equipment, except for aircraft, ships and boats	18,855	252,365	1,150	573,935	B
Sub-total D		217,500	959,612	87,427	1,207,438	

[a] See text for a description of the categories.

[b] Implied both from relevant regression coefficients and border-trade calculations.

TABLE 5.6
Ordinary Expansion Potential
(thousand US$)

SITC	Industry	Israeli exports 1978	Israeli imports 1978	Egyptian exports 1977	Egyptian imports 1977	Product category[a]
32[b]	Coal	0	1,017	2	70,626	B
58[b]	Plastic material	21,315	90,622	46	81,799	B
43[b]	Animal and vegetable oils and fats, processed, and waxes of animal or vegetable origin	66	•6,412	87	6,651	B
27[b]	Crude fertilisers, stone, sand, gravel et cetera	24,973	33,320	4,738	27,851	B
63[b]	Wood and cork manufactures	9,974	25,497	458	37,305	B
72	Electrical machinery and appliances	116,496	335,887	1,950	306,174	B
23[b]	Crude rubber	37	21,596	0	8,244	B
05	Fruits and vegetables	409,562	40,824	158,926	46,147	A
25[b]	Pulp and waste paper	0	23,303	0	17,188	B
24[b]	Wood, lumber and cork	7	65,935	1	248,629	B
21[c]	Fur, skins and hides	0	7,421	59	4,107	B
11	Beverages	5,708	5,492	27,073	2,584	A
52[b]	Mineral tar and crude chemicals from coal, petroleum, gas	254	278	193	639	C
41[c]	Animal oils and fats	154	409	4	67,006	B
93	Special transactions not classified according to kind	32,123	23,450	0	0	C
53[b]	Dyeing, tanning, colouring materials	1,370	23,644	116	57,914	B
011	Meat, fresh, chilled or frozen	28,166	52,837	380	57,914	B
612[b]	Manufactures of leather (also artificial)	465	2,671	1,826	5,090	B
22[c]	Oil seeds, oil nuts and oil kernels	11,417	111,749	10,699	15,605	B
26[b]	Silk, wool, cotton and other textile fibres	61,857	32,731	486,510	109,239	A
Sub-total E		723,944	905,095	693,068	1,167,442	

[a] See text for a description of the categories.
[b] Implied both from relevant regression coefficients and border-trade calculations.
[c] Implied only from border-trade calculations.

industries are characterised by a positive diversion and expansion potential. Their past trade performance in Egypt and Israel, as well as their sensitivity to geographic and economic distance, point in the 'right' direction. The list of potential Egyptian exports includes seven 2-digit and eight 3-digit industries. It includes the petroleum, textiles, clothing and aluminium industries, in which Egypt has a strong, proven export performance.

The list of Israel's export candidates is more varied. It includes rubber (mainly tyres), chemicals and metal manufactures, which are among the country's leading export industries. The list also contains, however, semi-tradeables like meat and meat preparations and milk and milk products. Trade in these perishables could be expanded substantially if the nearby markets were opened up to Egypt's and Israel's exporters.

Table 5.5 contains industries with a high expansion potential; that is, industries highly sensitive to geographic and economic distance. The list includes live animals and gas, which cannot easily be transported over long distances, as well as lime, cement, building and construction materials, including glass and clay, whose transportation costs become prohibitive over large distances. The list also contains less obvious candidates, such as paper, clothing, iron and steel, transport equipment, coffee, cocoa, tea and spices. These goods are traded widely in the international markets. It is somewhat surprising that they appear to be highly sensitive to geographic and economic distance. Some perishables such as fish are also found in the list.

Table 5.6 shows industries with an ordinary or normal expansion potential. These industries exhibit only marginal sensitivity to geographic and economic distance. The table contains a large and varied list, including some products in which the two countries trade heavily – fertilisers, electrical machinery, fruit and vegetables, organic chemicals and so on. These products are foot-loose; they exhibit no special sensitivity to either distance or border trade. This, however, does not mean that trade between neighbours is economically less desirable than trade with more distant partners.

The last columns in Tables 5.5 and 5.6 enable the reader to distinguish between different product categories. Products in which both Israel and Egypt are net exporters are labelled A. When both countries are net importers of a product, it is labelled B. In those cases where trade in one country or both is zero or where there are missing data, the product receives a C classification. Bearing in mind that both countries have a substantial overall trade deficit, it is not surprising that most industries listed in Tables 5.5 and 5.6 belong to the B category. It is not easy to predict the direction of net trade between Egypt and Israel in the products belonging to category A or B. It appears likely, however, that, at least in the short run, Israel will be a net exporter to Egypt of products such as meat, wood products, transport equipment, machinery, plastic materials and organic chemicals, while Egypt will be a net exporter of fish, sugar, clothing, cotton and textile fibres. These tentative predictions are based on the relative performance of the industries *vis-à-vis* the rest of the world. The economics of bilateral trade could well be quite different, especially after production patterns in both countries are given time to adjust to the new, post-war situation.

The figures are summarised in Tables 5.7 and 5.8. Trade diversion potential is presented in Table 5.7. The figures are obtained by adding up the appropriate totals from the last columns of Tables 5.3 and 5.4. Let us recall that the diversion potential is obtained by a two-stage procedure. In the first stage, net trade (that is, exports minus imports) is computed for each country. The smaller of the two figures is then chosen to represent the diversion potential. This procedure was applied to the figures in Table 5.3, which lists 'pure diversion' industries and Table 5.4, where the industries are considered to be candidates for both diversion and expansion. The totals, shown in Table 5.7, happen to be more or less equal for both Egypt and Israel.

TABLE 5.7
Summary of Diversion Potential

Direction of diversion	Value (thousand US$)	Relevant exports %	Relevant imports %
Israel to Egypt (A+C)	428,660	10.9	8.9
Egypt to Israel (B)	496,827	29.1	8.5

Actual diversion is, of course, likely to be much smaller than the maximum potential. Firms can be expected to divert their sales only if such a move increases their profits. They must also consider the costs of establishing marketing channels and other fixed transaction costs they are bound to incur in the process of switching from markets where they are already established to a hitherto unknown market in a recently hostile country. Only in those cases where transfer costs are high is substantial diversion likely to take place. It is therefore not surprising that the pure diversion potential appears to be relatively small in relation to total diversion potential. The relation between the two can be gauged by comparing the figures in Table 5.3, which shows pure diversion, with those in Table 5.4, where diversion and expansion potentials are indistinguishable. Relationships between diversion and expansion potentials are also exhibited in Table 5.8, where the different categories are summarised. For each country, diversion-cum-expansion is much larger than pure diversion. This indicates that both countries have a demonstrated advantage *vis-à-vis* the rest of the world mostly in products which are suitable candidates for bilateral trade between neighbouring countries – that is, products sensitive to geographic and economic distance.

TABLE 5.8
Summary of Trade Potential

	Israeli imports 1978	Israeli exports 1978	Egyptian imports 1977	Egyptian exports 1977
Diversion potential				
Israel to Egypt (A)	109,839	185,192	145,715	467
Diversion and expansion				
Israel to Egypt (C)	1,733,370	2,489,058	543,365	43,622
Total diversion potential				
Israel to Egypt (A+C)	1,843,209	2,674,250	689,080	44,089
Diversion potential				
Egypt to Israel	–	–	–	–
Diversion and expansion				
Egypt to Israel (B)	1,123,989	130,669	145,602	871,401
Expansion possibilities: direction unspecified				
(D+E)	1,915,830	890,321	2,390,163	765,212
Total of above				
(A+B+C+D+E)	4,883,028	3,695,240	3,244,845	1,680,702
Total trade	5,864,730	3,916,550	4,815,275	1,708,341
Percentage of above from total trade	83.3	94.4	67.0	98.4

A high proportion of total trade potential, however, is acccounted for by products having an expansion potential only. Their past performance is such that it is impossible to predict which of the two countries will be the net supplier, although the products themselves are candidates for trade between neighbours.

CONCLUSIONS

Predictions made by economists about potential bilateral trade between Egypt and Israel have usually been based on analyses of the two countries' past performance. Conceptually, this approach is useful for identifying only diversion potential. Figures of the kind shown in Table 5.8 confirm the intuitive notion that trade expansion could account for a high proportion of the total potential for trade between Egypt and Israel. It is conceivable, even likely, bearing in mind the discussion in Chapter 3, that trade potential between Israel and Egypt could be further extended to products not currently exported, or even currently manufactured, by either country.

Before peace was concluded between Israel and Egypt, all the trade of the former and nearly all the trade of the latter was conducted with overseas trading partners. All shipments required double handling and used either slow (ships) or very expensive (air) modes of transportation. This has restricted the volume of trade and limited the variety of tradeable goods and services. Most perishables were excluded from the tradeable sector, as were other goods characterised by high transport costs as well as service-intensive goods.

If Egypt's and Israel's exporters are allowed access to each other's markets on non-discriminatory terms, trade between the two countries is likely to exceed the level usually predicted, because traditional predictions tend to consider trade-diversion and to neglect trade-expansion potentials. Moreover, trade expansion is not limited to existing categories. If reasonably free trade is allowed to take place, it is likely to lead to a significant increase in the list of tradeable goods and services in both countries.

NOTES AND REFERENCES

1. These are usually ignored in conventional trade models.

2. See Herbert G. Grubel and Peter J. Lloyd, *Intra-Industry Trade* (New York: John Wiley, 1975), for a detailed discussion of border trade.

3. See Hans Linnemann, *An Econometric Study of International Trade Flows* (Amsterdam: North-Holland, 1966).

4. See Kindleberger, *Foreign Trade and the National Economy* (New Haven: Yale University Press, 1962) p. 11.

5. See Burenstam Linder, *op. cit.*

6. For a detailed analysis of these two factors, see Arad and Hirsch, 'Determination of Trade Flows and Choice of Trading Partners: Reconciling the Heckscher-Ohlin and Burenstam Linder Models of International Trade', *op. cit.*

7. The choice of OECD trade figures may be criticised as not fairly representing trade potential between Egypt and Israel. While our results may indeed be biased, it should be noted that although a high proportion of OECD trade consists of trade among industrialised countries, the figures include trade between industrialised and developing countries as well.

8. For a detailed analysis of the effect of trade barrier removal between neighbouring countries see Chapter 3.

9. These are the last years for which data were available. The Israeli trade data were taken from tapes supplied by the Israel Central Bureau of Statistics, Jerusalem; the Egyptian trade data, from tapes supplied by the United Nations Statistical Office.

10. Recall that we refer to negative values.

CHAPTER 6

Institutional Arrangements between Egypt and Israel

This chapter deals with the institutional framework within which economic relations between Egypt and Israel may develop. Here distinction is made between the short and long run. There is little doubt that at least in the near future these relations are going to be dominated by political considerations. Both parties are, of course, fully aware of the fact that peace between them is only the first, albeit supremely important, step towards a comprehensive settlement of the Arab-Israeli conflict. For the time being, therefore, as long as the prospects of a comprehensive settlement remain unclear, they are likely to refrain from taking steps implying long-term commitments, especially if these might create one-way dependence. They will also seek to preserve their existing relations with the rest of the world. This last point is especially relevant for Egypt, anxious as she is not to disrupt further her political and economic relations with the other Arab countries.

In the longer run, economic relations will be influenced by the nature of the peace settlement as well as the factors which normally affect economic relations between any pair of countries, such as their level of economic development, their relative abundance of complementary and competing resources and their policies towards international trade and investment.

Bearing in mind the overwhelming importance of the political considerations in shaping economic relations between Egypt and Israel, there is little sense in trying to outline alternative institutional frameworks which are unrelated to the political settlement. Since, however, such a settlement is not yet in sight, an essential ingredient is bound to be missing from the analysis. Rather then describing highly speculative scenarios, we chose to focus on two conceptually different frameworks. The first, developed in the present chapter, examines institutional arrangements available to the two parties in principle, taking into account existing trade and investment regimes in the world and the experience of other countries seeking to find a suitable framework for their economic relations. The alternative arrangements examined in this chapter are considered to be only marginally affected by the specifics of a comprehensive peace settlement in the Middle East.

117

In the concluding chapter, we deal with the short-run prospects for economic relations between Egypt and Israel, the short run being defined as the period preceding the establishment of a comprehensive peace.

DISCRIMINATION, INTEGRATION AND NORMALISATION

The Peace Treaty signed between Egypt and Israel in 1979 deals explicitly with economic relations between the parties in Article 2 of Annex III, which sets out the basis for these relations as follows:

1. The parties agree to remove all discriminating barriers to normal economic relations, and to terminate boycotts of each other upon completion of the interim withdrawal.

2. As soon as possible, and not later than 6 months after the completion of the interim withdrawal, the parties will enter negotiations with a view to conclude an agreement on trade and commerce for the purpose of promoting beneficial relations.[1]

The key concept dominating economic relations is the removal of discriminatory measures affecting bilateral transactions. Discrimination in international trade is a very old subject which has recently received much attention from scholars dealing with economic integration and cooperation.[2] It may be useful, therefore, to analyse briefly the relationship between the concepts of discrimination and integration.

Discrimination in international trade refers to the treatment that sovereign states reserve for goods and services originating in a given country in relation to similar goods originating in other foreign countries. It does not apply to the distinction that sovereign states make between goods originating in foreign countries and nationally-produced goods. Trading nations have, since the second half of the nineteenth century, adopted the tradition of rejecting discrimination (as defined here) as a matter of principle. The principle of non-discrimination towards third parties has been generally adopted and incorporated into bilateral as well as multilateral trade agreements.[3] More than 90 countries, handling over 90 per cent of world trade, recognise the validity of the MFN clause, which is the cornerstone of the existing international trade order, by adhering to the principles of the General Agreement on Tariffs and Trade (GATT). The concept is a general principle in law and can be formulated in different ways. The contracting parties (signatory countries) to the GATT adopted a very strict interpretation which stated:

'... Any advantage, favour, privilege or immunity granted by any contracting party to any product originating in or destined for any other country shall be accorded immediately and unconditionally to the like product originating in or destined to the territories of all other contracting parties' (Article I, paragraph 1).

The remaining articles of the GATT deal mainly with the application of the unconditional form of the MFN clause reproduced above and with some accepted exceptions to it. There are many possible sources of violation of the principle, but the GATT does not deal with all of them, in some cases because there is a consensus that nothing can be done about these violations. Boycotts for political or military reasons are examples of cases not dealt with by the GATT. Moreover, the GATT explicitly approves some forms of discrimination, when the signatory countries insist that other aims must take precedence over non-discrimination against fellow signatories to the GATT. A typical example is the position of the contracting parties concerning schemes for a customs union or a free trade area involving one or more members of the GATT (Article XXIV).

Integration in this context obliges those partners participating in the scheme to refrain from discrimination between home-produced goods and goods originating in member countries. The elimination of this kind of discrimination is considered by the GATT, in some cases, as a positive step, even if it leads to the emergence of a new kind of discrimination, namely that which distinguishes between goods which do and which do not originate in partner countries.

Having clarified the relations between discrimination and integration, certain questions must be considered. Does the normalisation of trade relations merely require removal of legal discrimination exercised against imports from and exports to the former enemy? Or should normalisation go beyond such a legalistic viewpoint, given that, in the case of recent enemies, more than 'normal' barriers hinder trade? Should not the parties take into account the psychological barriers to trade with the former enemy, given that 'normal' communication channels do not exist and will take time to develop? Is it reasonable to expect bilateral trade to develop at the same rate as trade between, say, two European countries, which do not have to consider unsettled major conflicts with other important parties but only comparative costs? It is reasonable to assume that none of the problems raised above can be taken care of merely by removing legal and bureaucratic obstacles to trade. Nor is it reasonable to expect that the proximity factor discussed at some length in Chapters 3 and 5 will, by itself, be sufficiently powerful to overcome the trade-inhibiting effects produced by thirty years of war between Egypt and Israel. Additional positive steps must be taken, if economic relations between the two countries are to become a reality within a reasonable time frame.

Having come to the conclusion that institutional, psychological and other barriers are likely to hinder the development of what might be termed normal economic relations between Egypt and Israel, let us consider a number of alternative frameworks which might be helpful in bringing about a mutually acceptable level of economic transactions.

The economic literature distinguishes among a number of basic types of cooperative frameworks compatible, under certain circumstances, with the basic principles of the GATT: preferential trade agreements, free trade areas, customs unions and common markets.

A preferential agreement between two trading partners is one according to which each offers the other partial tariff reductions on imports originating in the partner country. Reductions need not be linear. The preference margin can thus vary according to the tariff position considered. Preferential agreements are banned by the GATT, unless they can be considered as interim agreements leading to comprehensive forms of economic integration, like customs unions.

A free trade area covers a region in which individual member countries have abolished all barriers to trade originating in the other countries forming the free trade area. Each individual member country, however, is free to conduct its own trade policy with non-member countries.

A customs union stipulates that, in addition to the abolition of barriers to intra-area trade, members should establish a common external tariff to be applied to goods originating in non-member countries. Members must also agree on ways of sharing the income from the external tariff. The common external tariff, then, becomes the first instrument acquired by the union for the conduct of its common trade policy. The GATT accepts the formation of customs unions and free trade areas under certain conditions (Article XXIV).[4]

A common market goes beyond the liberalisation of intra-area trade in goods and services. Freedom of movement is also guaranteed to factors of production, including labour and capital originating in the area.

In the cases considered above, member countries may or may not belong to the same region. Both regional and non-regional integration schemes are allowed by the GATT, provided they comply with the conditions set out in the treaty. The liberal doctrine concerning the location of the members of the integration scheme contrasts sharply with the requirements concerning the coverage of goods by the agreement. Trade agreements covering only one branch of the members' economies (sectoral agreements) are not considered under Article XXIV of the GATT (referring to integration schemes), because they fail to cover substantially all the trade between the partners. Prospective partners to sectoral agreements are usually obliged to ask the GATT contracting parties for a waiver of obligations (Article XXV, paragraph 5).

The alternative arrangements discussed in the following sections fit into one or more of the general categories outlined above. In addition to considering their economic pros and cons, political feasibility and the implications for other international commitments of the parties are evaluated. The arrangements are ordered on the basis of the level of cooperation which they imply.

TRADE COOPERATION

The title 'Trade Cooperation' pertains to arrangements which come under the heading of 'classical' or 'conservative' trade diplomacy. The idea of trade cooperation is to establish a framework requiring cooperation at the government level only, with almost no room for private initiative. Annex III of the Peace Treaty between Egypt and Israel provides the legal basis for such an arrangement.

Bilateral trade and payments agreements based on such an approach would contain at a minimum the following elements.

1. The MFN rule, whereby each partner undertakes to treat the other's trade not less favourably than it does that of third parties: the inclusion of this provision cannot be viewed as a costly concession by either side, since both are contracting parties to the GATT and are therefore already bound by this rule. Apart from its symbolic value, this measure would preclude trade discrimination should either or both parties withdraw from the GATT.

2. A commitment of non-compliance with any past or future boycott against trade with the other party: this would require Egypt formally to renounce the Arab League boycott of Israel. It would also oblige each of the parties to refrain from adhering to possible future trade boycotts directed against one of them.

3. Sanitary regulations, such as the mutual acceptance of vaccination certificates: such regulations may well be important, given that farm produce, meat and fish, as well as livestock and processed foods, are likely to figure prominently in the trade of the two countries.

4. Provisions on transit trade, such as non-application of customs clearance procedures: this is particularly relevant, since both Egypt and Israel are coastal states bordering on two seas and possessing harbours

with extensive infra-structures for freight, storage and handling.

5. Provisions concerning payments for imports from the other country or exports to it: a typical requirement is that payments be made in a convertible currency or even in a single currency, such as United States dollars. Such provisions (that is, clearing arrangements) are often included in agreements between countries where one or both parties apply currency controls.

If Egypt and Israel were ready to consider more extensive cooperation, while excluding at the same time arrangements which might be viewed as leading to economic and political integration, they could opt for either one or both types of the following arrangements:

(a) joining a multilateral preferential trade club, either at the same time or at different points of time; or

(b) promotion of trade and cooperation in a limited region of their own territories.

The number of frameworks available for realisation of the scheme outlined under the first arrangement is rather limited, mainly because Israel is not considered to belong to the same category of states as Egypt and also because Israel does not maintain diplomatic relations with many Third World countries. The most obvious possibility would be to back or find ways of sponsoring initiatives by UNCTAD for extending cooperation among developing countries. This could be done by applying to Egyptian-Israeli trade the 1971 Protocol relating to Trade Negotiations among Developing Countries, signed under the auspices of the GATT. The Protocol, signed by a group of sixteen developing countries, including Egypt and Israel, called for the exchange of preferences covering a limited range of goods. Because of the state of war which existed between Egypt and Israel at the time, this provision did not apply to trade between them. The advantages of such an approach are two-fold. The framework already exists and it allows for further additions of tariff preferences on categories of commodities other than the ones already accepted by both countries and, perhaps more importantly, this framework, which has already received international sanction by the GATT and UNCTAD, could well be further developed in accordance with the decisions taken at the fifth session of the UNCTAD in May 1979 (Resolution 127 [V]). Each of the two countries could include in its own list commodities that are of special interest to each other.

The physical proximity between Egypt and Israel calls, as we have seen, for arrangements which facilitate bilateral economic cooperation. Border-trade agreements, free trade zones and joint export-processing zones come to mind within this context. Such institutional arrangements are not uncommon between neighbouring countries and need not have particular political significance. A legal basis for the promotion of border trade does in fact exist in Article XXIV, paragraph 3, of the GATT. This paragraph states that the rules of the GATT (mainly the MFN clause) need not be interpreted as preventing the granting by a contracting party of particular advantages or concessions to neighbouring countries in order to facilitate border trade. An arrangement could, for example, be envisaged for the El Arish-Rafa region, whereby free trade between this area and Israel would be permitted. Such an arrangement could make good economic sense, in view of the long distance between the region and the Nile Valley, where most of the economic activity of Egypt is centred.[5] A symmetrical proposal allowing duty-free trade between Eilat and Egypt could make the idea more acceptable politically. Because of Israel's geography, there would be no serious problem of customs control north of Eilat.

If such arrangements appear too ambitious from an economic or political point of view, more limited cooperation involving the setting up of joint free zones or export-processing zones in the above-mentioned regions might be considered. Free zones are geographic areas where raw materials, semi-processed goods and other inputs used in the production of exports can be imported by manufacturers on a duty-free basis. The granting of free-zone status is usually part of a series of special incentives designed to attract investors to areas or countries in which they would not otherwise invest. In general, free zones and especially those intended for export processing are located in areas that are easily accessible by sea or rail. They may include container facilities, shipyards, dry docks and warehouses. Activities to be developed in such zones include not only the storage of transit goods but also the manufacturing, processing, re-packing, sorting, blending and mixing of foods, as well as the processing of goods stored to supply local markets.

Free zones are often autonomous in the sense that a broad range of decisions is left to the boards of directors which, *inter alia*, build and maintain warehouses and supplies and provide services needed by the facilities operating in the zone. Investors thus usually face far less bureaucratic complications than in the domestic tariff area. From the customs' point of view, of course, the main provision is that goods exported from or imported into the zone are not subject to customs duties or other taxes, nor to the usual customs procedures. Moreover, equipment and machinery needed for operating the facilities located in the free zones are usually exempted from customs duties and other taxes. Business activities can be further encouraged by liberal provisions concerning taxes, financing and currency regulations.

Recent studies pertaining to the operation of free zones in several developing countries identify a number of typical free-zone industries, which include electronic components, optical instruments, electrical appliances, garments, toys, handicrafts and food processing, all products with high value and low weight.[6]

Trade relations can also be encouraged by bilateral preferential trade agreements which provide for mutual partial tariff reductions without extending them to third countries. Both Israel and Egypt have acquired some experience in such arrangements, since each has concluded a preferential agreement with the European Community (Israel in 1970 and Egypt in 1972). Israel's early agreements in 1964 and 1970 paved the way for the successful conclusion of the 1975 agreement, which provided for the establishment of a free trade area in manufactures.

There might, however, be difficulties in getting such a type of agreement approved by the contracting parties to the GATT, since it would conform neither to the rules set out in Article XXIV, paragraphs 4 to 10 (Customs Unions and Free Trade Areas), nor to those in Article XXV, paragraph 5 (Waivers). It could be claimed that other agreements encountered the same obstacles, but there was a fundamental difference in that one of the parties was the European Community, a major trading bloc accounting for a substantial share of world trade and having a major influence on GATT decisions.

It may well be worthwhile for both Israel and Egypt to invest substantial efforts in obtaining international approval for a partial preferential agreement, because of the advantages which such agreements offer. These agreements tend to preclude the decrease or elimination of tariff revenues, contrary to the case of free trade areas or customs unions. Theoretical analysis shows that tariff revenues may even increase, depending upon the tariff elasticities of import demand.[7] This element is important for a country such as Egypt, where the system of direct taxes is only partially developed and where tariff revenues finance a substantial portion of the national budget. Even in Israel, customs duties (including import levies) represented more than 10 per cent of total government income and nearly 20 per cent of the ordinary budget in recent years.

An additional advantage pointed out by Harry G. Johnson is that, if partner countries have a collective preference for industrialisation, partial preferential reductions on tariffs on industrial products allow for control over the distribution of trade diversion and trade creation.[8] This, in turn, implies that industrial exports of the partner country can increase at the expense of third countries' exports and not at the expense of its own domestic production. This seems a valid point in the case of Egypt and Israel. Since both countries are still in the midst of the industrialisation process, an exchange of minor preferences is an inexpensive way of reciprocally subsidising industrial exports by reserving a part of the market for the other party.

Preference agreements offer additional advantages in comparison with other integration schemes among developing countries in that by their very nature they do not lead to radical changes in resource allocation and do not, therefore, require complicated provisions for compensating mechanisms.[9]

ADVANCED FORMS OF INTEGRATION

More advanced forms of integration, such as a customs union or common market, appear to be ruled out for the foreseeable future, for both political and economic reasons. Even when comprehensive peace is achieved in the Middle East, it is difficult to conceive of circumstances in which economic integration based on the model of the European Community can make political or economic sense.

Integration is usually motivated by political as well as economic considerations. When proceeding beyond the reciprocal liberalisation of rules governing trade, investment and factor movement, integration usually implies giving up some degree of sovereignty and setting up of supra-national institutions empowered to establish rules for distributing the gains and the costs associated with the elimination of internal barriers to trade and factor movements.[10] It is inconceivable that the countries of the region will be able in the foreseeable future to overcome the difficulties inherent in formulating the principles of integration and in establishing the institutions needed to run the integrating economies, devising mechanisms for settling disputes and generally administering those sections of their economies which change from national to regional control.

Welfare considerations do not necessarily favour economic integration either. Customs union theory predicts that when economies characterised by complementary endowments and structures integrate, welfare losses due to trade diversion are likely to exceed welfare gains from trade creation. When endowments and structures of integrating economies are similar, gains from trade creation are likely to exceed losses from trade diversion.[11] The economies of Israel and Egypt are in many respects complementary rather than competitive.

On the other hand, there are the so-called dynamic gains, those due to economies of scale, to investor confidence, to proper division of labour between plants and sectors and to abolition of barriers between the countries.

On balance, it is difficult to predict whether welfare gains from a customs union or a free trade area encompassing Israel, Egypt and possibly additional Arab countries will exceed or be less than welfare losses. It is even more difficult to predict the distribution of gains and losses between the parties.

Given the differences in the levels of economic development and industrialisation, the levels and distribution of income, endowment of natural resources, the high degree of complementarity and, last but not least, the differences in the political regimes, economic integration based on the European Community model must be ruled out for the foreseeable future, even after outstanding political disagreements are settled.

While overall economic integration appears to be infeasible, more modest schemes allowing for close cooperation and division of labour could make both political and economic sense. This approach – the sectoral approach – is based on comprehensive economic integration covering a limited sector – that is, a single industry or a group of industries. The best known example of the sectoral approach is the ECSC, which preceded the European Community. The experience of the ECSC and its relevance to the Egyptian-Israeli situation are discussed in the following section.

SECTORAL APPROACH: THE ECSC

The idea of using partial economic integration as a means of achieving economic progress while solving or skirting political problems was successfully tried in Western Europe in the wake of World War II. A fundamental asymmetry in the political and economic objectives of France and West Germany characterised the relationship between these two recent belligerents. The historical animosity of the French towards the Germans had been reinforced by Germany's occupation of France during the war.[12] France was, moreover, concerned about the prospect of being surpassed industrially by West Germany as a result of the economic aid she was receiving from the United States.[13]

West Germany's objectives were different. She sought to avoid being incorporated into the Soviet bloc and she was therefore prepared to cooperate with the other Western powers in the establishment of multilateral frameworks which would safeguard her against isolation.[14] West Germany's other major priority was reconstruction and economic recovery.[15] This required access to West European markets and resources to replace the loss of East Germany.

While France was primarily interested in keeping West Germany weak, or at least tied to the West European framework, this objective was not shared by the United Kingdom or the United States, who were more concerned about the Soviet threat.[16] To overcome French resistance to bilateral cooperation, the Germans stressed the mutuality of economic interests, especially the natural complementarity with regard to iron, coal and steel production. To be successful, however, the initiative to integrate Western Europe had to come from France, not from Germany. As Dean Acheson, the United States Secretary of State at the time, observed, 'the key to progress towards integration is in French hands. In my opinion, France needs, in her own interest, to take the initiative rapidly and in a decisive way, if the character of West Germany is to be such as to allow for a healthy development in Western Europe'.[17]

French initiative did, indeed, materialise. It took the form of the Schuman Plan proposed by Jean Monnet, then the French Planning Commissioner. The plan called for the placing of all Franco-German production of coal and steel under a Common High Authority, in an organisation open to the participation of other European countries.[18] Such a measure, it was believed, would reduce considerably the possibility of war between the two former belligerents. It also diminished France's hopes for limiting West Germany's industrial development, something which France could not realistically hope to achieve anyway, given the opposition of the other Western allies, especially the United States.[19]

In addition to removing the basis for friction and rivalry that resulted from the 'absurd division' of this 'natural basin', both France and West Germany were expected to derive a number of advantages from the scheme:

(a) price stabilisation as a result of control over supply and demand, which would have a favourable effect on the market and would thus enhance investments;

(b) elimination of price discrimination, which had been a primary aim of France for decades, because German coal products had been sold at higher prices to foreign than to German steel producers;

(c) fuller exploitation of economies of scale in coal mining and in iron and steel production; and

(d) forestalling the establishment of private national or international cartels by stimulating competition among producers and by introducing strict anti-trust regulations.[20]

These objectives were incorporated into the Treaty of Paris, signed in 1951, which established the ECSC, a free trade area in coal and steel products among six countries (West Germany, France, Belgium, Luxembourg, the Netherlands and Italy).

According to Article 4, paragraph (a), of the Treaty of Paris, 'imports and exports duties, or taxes with an equivalent effect, and quantitative restrictions on the movement of coal and steel ... are recognized to be incompatible with the common market for coal and steel, and are, therefore, abolished and prohibited within the Community ... ' New customs duties on intra-regional trade were forbidden, as were subsidies on trade among members and restrictive business practices tending to segment the markets.

Subsequently, a series of agreements strengthening further economic relations between the West European countries were negotiated. These were accompanied by closer political ties which eventually led to the establishment of the European Community.

Looking back at this experiment with the sectoral approach, it is impossible to say whether the European Community did or did not inevitably follow the Coal and Steel Community. Its establishment might have been delayed or even avoided altogether had the ECSC been a failure or had the political circumstances been different. It is similarly impossible to say whether the ECSC would have survived, had the establishment of the European Community not followed. It can, however, be assumed that the founders of the ECSC must have considered it to be viable in its own right, since, at the time of its establishment, comprehensive integration could by no means be taken for granted.

The sectoral approach might also make sense in the context of peacemaking between Egypt and Israel. A possible application of the approach to the textiles and clothing industries of the countries is outlined in the concluding section.

SECTORAL APPROACH: THE TEXTILES AND CLOTHING SECTOR

The textiles and clothing sector was selected for the purpose of illustrating the application of the sectoral approach for a number of reasons.

(a) Both Egypt and Israel have relatively large textiles and clothing industries.

(b) There are interesting complementarities between the two countries' industries.

(c) The importance of foreign trade and the potential gains in the international competitive position of both countries from bilateral cooperation.

What follows is a short description of the Egyptian and Israeli textiles and clothing industries.

Textiles and clothing occupy a key position in Egypt's industrial sector. The industries employ about 300,000 workers, who account for a substantial proportion of total industrial employment. Output in 1979 exceeded $1,400 million of which about 20 per cent was exported, mostly to non-Western markets. Over two-thirds of the output was of yarn and cloth, produced mostly (about three-quarters) in state-owned enterprises. Output of clothing and wearing apparel, representing the balance, has been growing at a high rate. Private firms account for a high proportion of this sub-sector's output.

Cotton textiles and clothing also account for a high share of the country's manufactured exports. Cotton yarn is the country's major industrial export. Cotton cloth and other fabrics are also important export items. In recent years Egypt has also made progress in exporting clothes and other textile articles. Raw cotton was for decades the country's single most important export item. While the relative share of cotton has been declining, its share in total exports has remained high, as can be seen in Table 6.1.

Israel's textiles and clothing sector is much smaller in absolute and relative terms than Egypt's. In 1979, it employed fewer than 60,000 workers, who accounted for less than 20 per cent of total industrial employment. Gross output was about $1,200 million, of which nearly 30 per cent was exported, mainly to Western markets. While output in absolute terms has been growing in recent years, the share of the industry in manufactured value added and exports has been declining. Among the different sub-sectors, the share of yarn and cloth has been declining, while that of clothing has been growing at an impressive rate. Israel, like Egypt, is a cotton-growing country; the two countries hardly compete, however, since Egyptian cotton is of the long-staple variety, while Israel grows mainly medium-staple cotton.

The figures in Table 6.1, which shows the distribution of the two countries' international trade in 1979, indicate a fair degree of complementarity between the industries of Egypt and Israel. These complementarities could yield substantial gains to both countries, were they to pursue a policy of sectoral integration.

The first logical step, in the integration of the textiles and clothing industries of the two countries, is the elimination of trade barriers to facilitate unhampered intra-industry trade; that is, the free bilateral movement of raw materials, yarn, cloth, semi-finished and finished clothing, as well as services between the two countries.

The sectoral free-trade approach might be implemented in stages, taking into account adjustment difficulties. Consideration could be given to the different development levels of the two countries. This could be reflected in the length of the transition period granted to different sub-sectors. Moreover, the reduction in trade barriers need not be across the board and need not be

TABLE 6.1

Egyptian and Israeli International Trade in Textiles and Clothing, 1979
(million dollars)

SITC	Industry	Egypt Exports	%	Imports	%	Israel Exports	%	Imports	%
262	Wool and animal hair	8.2	1.2	12.0	10.9	8.7	1.9	16.6	7.2
263	Cotton	397.3	56.9	27.2	24.6	94.5	21.1	2.5	1.1
651	Textile yarn and thread	188.5	27.0	16.6	15.0	51.4	11.5	52.3	22.6
652	Cotton fabric (woven)	58.6	8.4	–		9.4	2.1	24.7	10.6
653	Textile fabrics (woven, not cotton)	–		10.0	9.1	11.1	2.5	55.8	24.1
656	Made-up articles (textile)	6.9	1.0	1.8	1.6	20.1	4.5	14.0	6.0
841	Clothing (not fur)	8.2	1.2	5.2	4.7	198.7	44.5	23.5	10.1
	Other textiles and clothing (from SITC groups 26, 65, 84)	30.6	4.3	37.7	34.1	53.2	11.9	42.4	18.3
Total		698.3	100.0	110.5	100.0	447.1	100.0	231.8	100.0

SOURCES: For Israel, *Foreign Trade Statistics Quarterly*, Central Bureau of Statistics, Jerusalem, no. 4, 1980; for Egypt, *Foreign Trade Statistics 1979*, Central Agency of Manpower Statistics and Mobilization, Cairo, 1980.

A dash denotes negligible, that is less than one half million dollars.

equal. External tariffs do not necessarily have to be harmonised, although in this case, it might be necessary to establish rules of origin and a mechanism for administering these rules. Considering, however, that the idea is to develop trade in inputs, while exporting final products mainly to third countries, rules of origin could be quite liberal.

If the measures outlined here are considered too far-reaching, other less comprehensive arrangements might be introduced. Israel could introduce offshore assembly provisions or 'free zones' of the kind provided for in the tariff legislations of the United States and the European Community. These provisions would be applied to goods manufactured in Egypt's free zones. Israeli tariffs on finished products might be levied only on the value added offshore.[21] Such measures could help to promote trade in semi-finished and finished clothing.

Initially, the establishment of a sectoral free trade agreement in textiles and clothing is likely to lead to a high level of intra-industry trade between independent firms. In the longer run, the principal method of cooperation will probably be in the form of direct investments by the firms of one country in the other, setting up subsidiaries which are integrated with the parent company, as well as different forms of joint ventures. These are more advantageous than mere trade and looser forms of cooperation because they facilitate closer coordination and more efficient utilisation of centralised functions such as marketing, design and quality control.

The strategy of establishing manufacturing operations, which draw on the competitive advantage of the two countries, may be attractive not only to Egyptian and Israeli firms. Firms from other countries such as the United States or Japan, which have no free trade agreement with the European Community, as well as European firms, may also wish to capitalise on the opportunities offered by combining the advantages of Egypt and Israel.

An agreement along the lines outlined above is unlikely to affect trade in cotton, since trade barriers are already low or nil in both countries. Israeli experts, however, do expect some imports of long-staple cotton, in order to produce high quality yarns and fabrics (such as poplins).

Exports of synthetic fibres from Israel to Egypt appear to have good prospects in the short run, given the high Egyptian duties. Egypt's production of crude oil, however, may enable her to become competitive in the production of synthetic fibres, while Israel, depending as she does on imported oil, would tend to lose her comparative advantage.

Prospects for Egyptian exports of fine unfinished cotton yarn (grey) to Israel appear to be promising, particularly if Israel eliminates not only duties but also obligatory payments. In turn, Egypt, since she is rapidly expanding her weaving capacity, could provide a market for Israel's synthetic yarns. Israel would clearly benefit from this diversion of trade.

Intensive two-way trade can be expected in such branches as knitted and crocheted goods and in the clothing industry in general. Where fashion is not a factor (for example, in underwear) prospects for Egyptian exports are promising. Although the Israeli consumer market is quite small, it could provide Egyptian producers with the opportunity of testing their products in preparation for entry into larger and even more sophisticated markets.

Israel can expect to export high-fashion clothing (for example, ladies' suits) destined for the Egyptian high-income groups, because trade barriers in this class of products are particularly high and because imported clothing is considered desirable by certain consumers. It might also prove profitable to tap the large Egyptian market in less expensive and fashion-sensitive products, such as pantihose, blouses, T-shirts and jeans, all items in which Israel has gained considerable experience.

In conclusion, the textiles and clothing industries in Egypt and Israel exhibit such a wide range of potential complementarities that cooperation between them may yield very substantial dividends in the form of a strong competitive position for both countries' industries in existing and new markets, as well as in existing and new lines of business. It could, indeed, make sense for the governments of the two countries to promote cooperation by making suitable institutional arrangements which will facilitate easier movement of goods, processes, capital and know-how between enterprises in the textiles and clothing industries. Such a policy is bound to improve the competitive position and export performance of the industries of both countries. It is also likely to contribute to an increase in investments from both domestic and foreign enterprises.

Being less comprehensive than a common market or even a free trade area, the sectoral approach is also less risky. It may be applied to a sector or sectors where the chances of success are high, where the costs of failure are low and where the potential for conflict over the distribution of costs and gains is small. It might, in short, be used as a test case, an experiment in economic cooperation between nations which had no experience in cooperation of any kind before.

NOTES AND REFERENCES

1. Treaty of Peace between Israel and the Arab Republic of Egypt, Instrument of Ratification, Government Information Center, Jerusalem, 1979, Annex III, p. 1.

2. See, for example, Fritz Machlup, *A History of Thought on Economic Integration* (London: Macmillan, for the International Economics Association, 1977).

3. See John H. Jackson, *World Trade and the Law of GATT* (New York: McGraw-Hill, 1969). The author asserts that early versions of the principle can be traced back as far as the fourteenth century.

4. These conditions, contained in Article XXIV, paragraphs 5 to 9, of the GATT, refer, *inter alia*, to the need for presenting a plan and a programme of the integration process.

5. It might, however, be objected to on political grounds.

6. See David Wall, 'Export Processing Zones', *Journal of World Trade Law*, Twickenham, United Kingdom, September-October 1976, pp. 478-87.

7. See Tovias, *Théorie et Pratique des Accords Commerciaux Préférentiels* (Bern: Herbert Lang, 1974) chs II and III.

8. See Johnson, 'An Economic Theory of Protection, Tariff Bargaining and the Formation of Customs Unions', *Journal of Political Economy*, June 1965, pp. 256-83. The free trade areas and customs unions are, on the other hand, based on formulae which imply that the partner countries have no control over the mix of trade diversion and trade creation. By their very nature, they are all-or-nothing propositions.

9. It should be remembered that failure to agree on the operation of compensation mechanisms has been a major reason for the failure of customs unions and common markets among developing countries, as in the case of the East African Community (EAC). For an assessment of the problems confronted by the EAC leading to its ultimate disintegration, see Peter Robson, 'The New Setting for Economic Cooperation in East Africa', in Robson (ed.), *International Economic Integration* (Harmondsworth: Penguin Books, 1972) pp. 426-35; and Arthur Hazlewood, *Economic Integration: the East African Experience* (New York: St Martin's Press, 1975).

10. On this point, see Hugh Corbet, 'One Course of Recovery for an Ailing European Community', *The World Economy*, London, March 1981, pp. 57–68. Following Johnson, Corbet argues that most of the economic benefits from integration can be derived by all parties following a policy of liberalisation. Setting up of supra-national organisations and giving up national sovereignty is superfluous. This argument is, however, unlikely to be valid in cases where the integrating economies are characterised by substantial differences in the level of economic development and internal economic regimes as in the case under consideration.

11. See James E. Meade, *The Theory of Customs Unions* (Amsterdam: North-Holland, 1955); and Richard G. Lipsey, 'The Theory of Customs Unions: a General Survey', *Economic Journal*, London, 1960, pp. 496-513.

12. General de Gaulle's declaration on 13 October 1945 sums up quite well the attitude of the French: 'We have been three times invaded by Germany in a single lifetime. We do not want to see a Reich anymore.' Quoted in *Keesing's Contemporary Archives*, Bristol, 8-15 December 1945, p. 7595.

13. See Alfred Grosser, *Les Occidentaux* (Paris: Fayard, 1978) pp. 89 and 106.

14. See J.K. Sowden, *The German Question, 1945-1973* (New York: St Martin's Press, 1975) pp. 30-31, referring to Konrad Adenauer's view on Franco-German solidarity as a bulwark against Soviet expansion.

15. See H. Bohrer, 'Die deutsch-französichen Wirtschaftsbeziehungen und die Möglichkeiten ihrer zukunftigen Gestaltung', in *Europa-Archiv*, Viertes Jahr, July-December 1949, pp. 2549-56; and the special number of *Der Volkswirt*, Beilagen, no. 10, 1956, devoted to French-German cooperation.

16. France sought to convince the other Allies in the early post-war years to adopt the following policies: precluding the setting up of a central government; converting the Länder (regions) into key

political units of a future German entity; requiring that the French-controlled zone and the Saarland be economically integrated into France; requiring the internationalisation of the Ruhr, while limiting industrial activities in that region; dismantling certain giant corporations (such as Thyssen). See Sowden, *op. cit.*, pp. 27, 87-88 and 91-92.

17. Dean Acheson, *Foreign Relations of the United States,* Diplomatic Papers (Washington: US Government Printing Office, 1949) p. 470; translated back into English from the French translation in Grosser, *op. cit.*, p. 154.

18. See Paul Reuter, *La Communauté Européenne du Charbon et de l'Acier* (Paris: Librairie Générale de Droit et de Jurisprudence, 1953) p. 4, where Robert Schuman, then Foreign Minister of France, in a preface to the book, reproduces his own Declaration.

19. The Plan would have the advantage of displacing the previously established Ruhr authority, an organisation which was supposed to allocate the Ruhr's output of coal, coke and steel between German exports and domestic use and which had created a lot of ill-feelings in Germany, while leaving France dissatisfied with the degree of control over Germany's cartelised industries. On this subject, see Henry Rieben, *Des Ententes de Maîtres de Forges au Plan Schuman* (Lausanne: Centre de Recherches Européennes, 1970) p. 324. See also Reuter, *op. cit.*, pp. 19-22, and Louis Lister, *Europe's Coal and Steel Community* (New York: Twentieth Century Fund, 1960) p. 8.

20. The idea of linking French and German heavy industries was quite old, having been proposed already in 1914 by the future Prime Minister of France, Paul Reynaud. See Machlup, *op. cit.*, p. 169. On the European coal and steel question, see Jacques L'Huillier, *Théorie et Pratique de la Coopération Économique Internationale* (Paris: Génin, 1957); and Kent Jones, 'Forgetfulness of Things Past: Europe and the Steel Cartel', *The World Economy,* London, May 1979. For a systematic review of the origins of the Plan, see William Diebold Jr, *The Schuman Plan* (New York: Praeger, 1959).

21. See Donald B. Keesing and Martin Wolf, *Textile Quotas against Developing Countries,* Thames Essay No. 23 (London: Trade Policy Research Centre, 1980) p. 33.

CHAPTER 7

Short-term Perspectives on Economic Relations

The alternative institutional arrangements concerning economic relations between Egypt and Israel discussed in Chapter 6 assume some kind of bilateral preferences. Preferences imply, however, discrimination against third parties – that is, against countries not included in the preferential arrangements. While such arrangements need not be ruled out some time in the future, they are unlikely to be feasible in the short run, for political reasons. As long as an agreement on the Autonomy seems remote and, perhaps more importantly, as long as other Arab countries fail to join the peace process, Egypt and Israel are unlikely to enter into preferential agreements even if they offer both parties substantial economic gains. Economic relations based on mutual preferences could be part of a wider peace agreement between Israel and her neighbours. Until progress in this direction is achieved, the most likely framework for bilateral economic relations is one of non-discrimination; that is, a framework of economic relations whereby the principle of MFN treatment is maintained. This chapter examines the prospects of economic relations between Egypt and Israel within this type of framework.

POLITICAL CONSIDERATIONS

There is little doubt that uncertainty about the future of the political relations, which stems from lack of progress on the Autonomy issue and the refusal of other Arab countries to join in the peace process, inhibits further expansion of Egyptian-Israeli economic relations and prevents them from reaching what might be termed their 'natural level'. As long as the present level of uncertainty remains, business firms in both countries are likely to be hesitant about committing the resources required to realise the potential for bilateral trade and investment.

It is unlikely that economic considerations, especially those pertaining to the opportunity losses associated with failure to realise the potential gains from trade and investment, will be of decisive importance in impelling the governments towards a settlement of their political differences. Both parties are committed, however, to the peace process and they realise that economic relations are an important tangible demonstration of their political intentions towards each other. Thus both countries publicly support 'normalisation', of which economic relations are an important component.

Egypt and Israel have conflicting views, however, about the desired volume of bilateral transactions. This conflict ought to be recognised and understood at the outset. Israel wishes, for political reasons, to expand the scope of economic relations, whereas Egypt is interested in minimising it. Israel's attitude is easily understood. The peace agreement obliges her to return to Egypt territories which have considerable strategic and economic importance. The Sinai Peninsula contains oil and other minerals and has in recent years become a source of tourist income. More important still is its military significance, since it provided Israel with an irreplaceable strategic hinterland. All these real assets were surrendered in return for the peace agreement which, although tremendously significant, is after all only a declaration of intent.

From Israel's point of view, economic transactions, such as trade, investments and movement of people, goods and services, provide the concrete contents of the peace. Without such flows, peace remains as empty and fragile shell which can be easily broken.

The Egyptians have a different point of view. By making peace with Israel they have granted that country something it had been denied since its establishment: formal recognition by its largest adversary, who had taken a leading role in all the Arab-Israeli wars. In return, so argue the Egyptians, Israel has given back to Egypt territories which had been hers in the first place. The 'Palestinian question', which has always been and remains the core of the Arab-Israeli conflict, remains unsolved. Establishment of friendly relations between Egypt and Israel, of which close economic relations are but one aspect, must according to this view be preceded by noticeable progress on the Palestinian question. The Egyptians support their arguments by referring to the economic losses which they suffer, due to the disruption of diplomatic relations with most of the Arab states and the economic sanctions imposed on them following the signing of the Peace Treaty.

Another issue ought to be clarified in this context. Arab sanctions against Egypt apply to official aid, which, indeed, has been discontinued. Private transactions, however, have been only marginally affected and the Egyptians wish, for obvious reasons, to continue being the recipients of private capital inflows from the Gulf States and other Arab countries. They, like their European, Japanese and even North American counterparts, explain their reluctance to engage in more intensive transactions with Israeli firms by their fear of losing some of the lucrative business with the Gulf States, where the Arab boycott against Israel is allegedly still enforced.

Actual economic relations between Egypt and Israel are fashioned by policies which represent some sort of a compromise between these conflicting views. The compromise, however, inevitably favours the Egyptian view. This is so since, whenever the two parties disagree on the volume of bilateral transactions between them, the party which seeks to minimise the volume is of course in a more powerful position as a rule. It is difficult to force this party to buy or sell more than it wishes. Thus it is the Egyptians who decide in fact on the upper bounds of the volume of transactions with Israel. It is up to the Israelis or third parties to persuade them that it is in their interest to increase the scope and volume of economic transactions.

Partial success in this direction is represented by the Egyptian-Israeli oil agreement which was incorporated into the economic provisions of the Peace Treaty.[1] It provides a clear example of a politically motivated transaction which could have a profound effect on future economic relations between the two countries. The oil agreement negotiated in 1979 provided for the sale of substantial quantities of oil by Egypt to Israel, ostensibly to replace the oil which Israel had previously pumped from the oil wells she held and partially developed in the Sinai. Its significance from Israel's point of view lay, at least partly, in the fact that it obliged Egypt to enter publicly into a long-term agreement with the former enemy. Economically, the agreement is not of great significance since there is a ready world market for oil and since the transactions are based on world market prices. Nevertheless, the oil agreement has benefited both countries: it provides Egypt with a reliable market and Israel with a steady and close supplier. Both sides presumably share the savings in transport costs in an equitable manner. While the oil agreement between Egypt and Israel appears to be satisfactory *per se*, it leads to a substantial deficit in Israel's current account with Egypt, since trade in other goods and services has been quite small. This imbalance in Israel's bilateral current account might, at least partially, be corrected by adopting the compensation principle; that is, enabling Israel to pay for all or part of the oil with goods and services rather than with convertible currency. Barter, as is well known, is not a very efficient way of distributing the gains from international exchange. It is quite common, however, especially when politically-sensitive transactions are involved and Egypt, moreover, has barter arrangements in many of her international transactions, especially with the countries of the Eastern bloc. If the principle of trading oil against goods is accepted, then two-way trade between Egypt and Israel can reach several hundred million dollars in a short time frame. In the absence of such an arrangement the Egyptian-Israeli trade balance is likely to be in favour of the former for some years to come.

NATURE OF BILATERAL TRANSACTIONS

Pure trade, that is trade which is unrelated to other forms of international transactions, need not necessarily dominate relations between Egypt and Israel even in the short run. Substantial flows of additional trade could be generated through transactions involving some form of direct investment – that is, transactions labelled in Chapter 3 as export or output creation.

Output creation was defined as a new economic activity made possible by access to hitherto closed markets. Export creation, unlike output creation, is not a new activity. It is likely, however, to require capital outlays to facilitate expansion of output needed to service the new export market.

Export and output creation are facilitated, as shown in Chapter 3, by the physical proximity between Egypt and Israel, which makes it possible to reduce transfer costs of inputs as well as of finished products. Proximity thus can lead to the expansion of the list of tradeable goods and services in both countries. Moreover, goods and services produced in one country, and containing inputs originating in the other, might become exportable to third countries.

Such an expansion of the tradeable sector requires, however, long-term commitment of capital and managerial resources which are very scarce in Egypt. Israeli firms seeking to do business in Egypt thus often face the requirement of transferring know-how and providing services, credit and even long-term capital to their prospective clients. Since such transfers usually require close and continuing relations between the transacting parties, they often lead to the establishment of joint ventures and other forms of partnerships.

The potential for investment-related trade between Egypt and Israel is further enhanced by recent developments in the Egyptian economy. The Egyptian national product has been expanding at a high rate since the late 1970s. Expansion has been accompanied, and to some extent facilitated, by a substantial increase in foreign-exchange inflows from oil, tourism, Suez Canal fees, workers' remittances from abroad and foreign aid. These flows, which by 1980 had reached about $10,000 million, reduced but did not eliminate Egypt's current balance deficit. They more than made up the loss of income from the withdrawal of Arab aid in retaliation for Egypt's decision to make peace with Israel.

The increase in income, however, was not fully matched by expansion of productive capacity. Consequently the economy's growth has been constrained by bottlenecks in the country's infra-structure, public services and productive capacity in a growing number of sectors, as well as a continuing shortage of foreign exchange.

The supply bottlenecks which characterise the Egyptian economy affect not only the country's import-substituting industries; they equally affect its actual and potential exportables. In the short term, Egypt simply does not have the productive capacity needed to take care of domestic requirements, let alone exports. Thus she imports goods and services in which she clearly enjoys a long-term comparative advantage. She is a net importer of many fruits, vegetables and dairy products, cement, iron and steel, textiles and clothing and numerous other goods, which she is potentially well placed to produce on a competitive basis in the longer run, once productive capacity is sufficiently expanded.

The government has been anxious to reduce the country's dependence on imports by relieving some of the bottlenecks described above. To achieve this goal, the government has given high priority to investments in construction, industry and agriculture. Business firms, including foreign firms, are encouraged to participate in this endeavour by tax concessions, liberal import rules and other regulations regarding transfer of earnings, subsidised loans and other incentives.

Thus investment-related rather than pure trade may well dominate the international transactions with Egypt for some time to come. Firms which will manage to combine trade with investment or trade with the provision of needed technological and managerial know-how are likely to find a more ready market than firms which limit themselves to pure trade.

BUSINESS ENVIRONMENT

Trade, whether 'pure' or 'investment-related', is normally carried out by business enterprises which respond to what they perceive as risks and opportunities inherent in the different markets. Both opportunities and risks are, in turn, affected to an important degree by the formal rules and regulations pertaining to trade, investment and other business transactions which constitute the economic relations between any pair of countries.

Formally, economic relations between Egypt and Israel are conducted within the framework of the Agreement on Trade and Commerce signed on 8 May 1980. The avowed objective of the agreement is to facilitate normalisation of relations between the two countries. It stipulates that each party should accord the other MFN treatment. Both parties agree to comply with each other's sanitary rules and recognise the other party's certificates issued by the 'relevant authorities'. The agreement calls on each party to allow the other to participate in fairs and exhibitions. It provides for payments in convertible currencies and sets up a bilateral commission to discuss questions concerning implementation of the agreement. Trade conducted within the framework of preferential agreements signed by the parties is, however, exempted from the MFN rule. Thus Egypt may continue to give preferences to Arab countries and other developing countries, while Israel continues to give preferences to the members of the European Community. The text of the agreement is reproduced in Appendix 3.

In a country such as Egypt not too much significance can be attached to a formal agreement which states that this or that foreign country will benefit from MFN treatment. If public sector firms, which control a high proportion of total imports, are explicitly or implicitly instructed to refrain from doing business with certain suppliers, the latter will find that very little business comes their way, regardless of whether they are competitive or not. It is consequently not easy to say whether the fact that Israel's exports to Egypt in 1981, which totalled less than $20 million (as compared with oil imports, estimated at $400 million), is due to political or economic reasons.

In the latter months of 1981, public sector firms were given official permission to import from Israel. It is to be expected that this change in policy plus the fact that Israeli and Egyptian firms acquired some experience in doing business with each other, as well as the psychological impact of Israel's withdrawal from the rest of Sinai in the spring of 1982, would combine to reduce further the barriers to trade between the two countries.

We have stated repeatedly that transactions between Egypt and Israel enjoy potential competitive advantage over transactions with third countries due to savings in transfer costs. This proximity factor could encourage trade, especially in transport-intensive and other service-intensive goods which are characterised by relatively high transport costs. Realisation of this advantage has been hindered in practice by the Egyptian rule which stipulated that Egyptian vehicles must carry all goods transported overland in Egypt. This rule meant that overland shipments from Israel to Egypt had to be trans-shipped at the border. The costs involved reduced, and in some cases completely nullified, the cost advantage inherent in border trade between the two countries. Changes in this rule and an agreement on overland transportation which came into effect at the end of April 1982 will undoubtedly increase the attractiveness of bilateral trade.

Another formidable trade barrier is represented by the complicated rules and regulations governing imports into Egypt. Particularly cumbersome in this respect are the rules concerning the allocation of foreign exchange, which vary between product groups and over time, as the classification of goods and hence their effective price changes. Some of these trade barriers could be lowered if Egypt and Israel were to sign a trade and payments agreement which would specify the quantities and value of goods to be exchanged and the method of payment.

Additional encouragement to trade could be given by a clearing agreement which would provide for bilateral credit, specify terms and method of payment and allow Egyptian and Israeli suppliers to accept payment in each other's rather than only in convertible currencies. Egypt has a long history of barter and barter-like agreements with East European and developing countries. Buy-back arrangements or so-called counter-trade could also be contemplated. Under such arrangements, the party which expects to have a positive bilateral trade balance undertakes to accept a specified volume of goods or services, offered by the other party, in full or partial payment for its own exports. Egyptian-Israeli trade could well be further enhanced if it were conducted within the framework of such an agreement.

As in the case of the oil agreement discussed above, it is easy to show that arrangements of the kind proposed here are not the best way of boosting trade. They lead to distortions in the allocation of resources and hence to economic waste. Critics of the idea must realise, however, that the alternative to a trade and clearing agreement is likely to be severe restrictions on trade and rationing of foreign exchange. Under these circumstances a trade and clearing agreement may well turn out to be a superior alternative.

ARRANGEMENTS REQUIRING INTERNATIONAL COOPERATION

Third parties, both international organisations and individual countries, could help to boost Egyptian-Israeli economic relations in a number of ways which are outlined below.

Egypt and Israel receive fairly substantial aid from abroad, especially from the United States. Israeli exports to Egypt could be increased by allowing Israeli firms to bid on aid-financed contracts involving Egypt. Egyptian exports to Israel could likewise benefit from arrangements of this type. Such arrangements would not only increase the scope and volume of bilateral trade, they would also diminish the trade-diversion costs inherent in any programme of tied aid. Recipients of aid funds in both countries would have a wider range of goods from which to choose. Transfer costs are likely to play an important role in affecting the delivered costs of different supplies. Goods originating in the donor countries which may be cheaper than Egyptian or Israeli goods on an ex-factory basis may be more expensive when delivered to the customer or final user, considering freight, insurance, handling and other transfer costs. Egyptian-Israeli trade may also be enhanced by certain arrangements with the European Community. Both countries have trade and cooperation agreements with the Community, within the framework of its Mediterranean Policy launched in 1972. The two countries therefore already have some kind of a common framework involving their economic relations with the European Community.

Despite the mixed reactions which the Peace Treaty encountered in the European Community, it should be noted that the Political Commission of the European Parliament on 3 April 1979 issued a strongly-worded statement not only endorsing the agreement but also asking the Commission of the Community to take concrete steps to promote industrial cooperation between Israel and Egypt.[2] The two countries could therefore base their dealings with the Community on this political statement.

Tariff concessions applied by the European Community to imports from countries with which the Community has free-trade-area or other types of agreements apply only to goods originating in the signatory countries. When products imported from such countries contain inputs purchased from third countries the product may be subject to tariffs. These rules of origin could be re-interpreted when applied to Egypt and Israel to allow tariff-free access to goods manufactured in either party, even when they contain inputs imported from the other country.

This type of provision is contained in the second Lomé Convention, negotiated in 1980, concerning the trade of the European Community with fifty-eight developing countries, mostly in Africa, the Caribbean and the Pacific. Similar proposals have in fact been made in the context of the Euro-Arab Dialogue.[3] This approach could have additional merits in that it would constitute a step towards multilateralisation of the Community's Mediterranean Policy, which thus far has consisted of a mosaic of bilateral agreements between the Community and Mediterranean countries. These agreements are based on disparate models, although the approach is common. For example, the Community's agreement with Israel is very similar to agreements the Community signed with the individual member countries of the European Free Trade Association (EFTA) in 1972. On the other hand, the main trade concession granted by Egypt to the Community, in return for the concessions she was granted, is the application of the MFN rule to imports from the Community. This stipulation is of little practical importance, since Egypt, as an established member of the GATT, is obliged in any case to refrain from discriminating between her trading partners.

An agreement of the kind outlined above could be more easily accepted by the European Community if Israel were to offer reciprocal rights to the Community (and Egypt), since Israel's relations with the Community are based on the principle of reciprocity. Such an arrangement would present an additional advantage for Egypt, in that her products could be exported to the Community for further processing and re-exported to Israel. Such triangular trade is likely to be of particular relevance to Greece, which joined the Community on 1 January 1981, and to Italy. In fact, the Cooperation Agreement between Egypt and the Community contains a provision calling for special emphasis on regional cooperation in the Mashrek. When the agreement with Egypt was signed, it was stressed that Community aid would be important in encouraging trilateral cooperation between oil-exporting countries, Egypt and the Community.[4] These points suggest that the Community does not regard the agreement with Egypt as a strictly bilateral instrument but also as a means for promoting trilateral cooperation involving other countries in the Middle East.

Thus, while the signatories of the agreement between the European Community and Egypt are unlikely to have had the Egyptian-Israeli peace in mind when they formulated the provisions regarding trilateral cooperation, the framework decided upon could, with few modifications, be adapted to the new situation.

CONCLUDING REMARKS

In this chapter we sought to show how economic relations between Egypt and Israel can be enhanced in the short run, thereby contributing to a minimal degree of interdependence between the two countries, even before a comprehensive Arab-Israeli peace settlement is reached.

The problem with interdependence between any pair of countries, let alone between recent belligerents, is that it is difficult to plan and control. This is so partly because of the complex way in which individual transactions, often decided upon by businessmen interested in making profits, add to the cost of dissociation, which can lead to one-way dependence and which, when incurred, must be borne by the entire community. Consequently there may well be divergence between private and public interests where the private interests, more often than not, are in favour of expanding further bilateral transactions and the public interest is best served by curtailing them.

It should be borne in mind, however, that the public interest is not necessarily to prevent the cost of dissociation from exceeding a certain level; it is to prevent relative costs of dissociation from changing in a direction which will alter the relationship between the two countries from interdependence to one-way dependence. Since each transaction adds to the cost of dissociation of both countries, monitoring and control become rather complicated.

It is only rarely that the incremental decisions of individual businessmen lead to a strongly asymmetrical build-up of one country's cost of dissociation. It is therefore common, under normal conditions, for market economies to entrust a high proportion of their international transactions to individual firms. Even market economies do, however, adopt special policies regarding so-called strategic materials. Their governments tend to intervene also in large-scale transactions involving non-market economies whose trade and other economic transactions are highly centralised and are often motivated by political considerations. It is only sensible to add to this list transactions between recent or, for that matter, potential belligerents.

The common denominator which all these cases have is the cost of dissociation. This cost can rightly be ignored when there are alternative suppliers or markets. It can also be ignored when political and economic relations between trading partners are such as to make dissociation unthinkable. When dissociation is a distinct possibility, the government, even in market economies, has a legitimate concern with the volume, composition and terms of the transactions with the country in question.

Recent belligerents, seeking to stabilise a fragile peace between them, cannot afford to ignore these factors. If they do they may find that their economic relations lead to instability and create conflict and damage rather than enhance economic vested interest in peace, which bilateral transactions, if properly handled, can promote.

Actual interdependence, as represented by the level of bilateral transactions as well as the absolute and relative cost of dissociation of both countries, could in time be so high as to make dissociation unacceptable to both sides. If this level is reached, one can speak of irrevocable interdependence, a concept introduced in Chapter 2.

Robert Schuman must have had this kind of interdependence in mind when, in May 1950, he proposed the establishment of the ECSC, which, in his view, would eventually make 'any war between France and Germany not only unthinkable but materially impossible'.[5] Franco-German reconciliation took place, however, under exceptional circumstances, where one country, Germany, was totally defeated and where both countries, as well as the rest of Western Europe, felt threatened by the Soviet Union. Even so, the creation of the ECSC, of Euratom and of the European Community, which were supposed to foster interdependence in the sense mentioned above, took years to accomplish.

To become irrevocable, interdependence must be far-reaching; it must involve giving up the right to unilateral decisions on matters such as trade, investment, taxation and movement of production factors. Recent belligerents are unlikely to possess the mutual trust needed to take such far-reaching steps, which few sovereign countries are willing to take under any circumstances. The degree of common interest and of mutual trust needed to renounce dissociation as an instrument of bilateral economic relations need not, however, be high. It is up to the governments to make sure that the probability of dissociation is sufficiently low to be neglected by the business community. It is also up to the governments to devise the institutions, rules and regulations which will ensure that the cost of dissociation will not depart from an acceptable ratio. If the governments fulfill these functions, then the business sector can be counted on to commit the resources which will gradually lead to the desired level of interdependence.

In Chapter 1 we introduced Professor Boulding's concepts of the threat, exchange and integration systems which govern both inter-personal and international relations. It is appropriate to conclude the book by quoting mathematician and psychologist Anatol Rapoport, who, in commenting on Professor Boulding's three systems, made the following observations:

'...in a threat system ... each party would prefer it if the other were not there ... in an exchange system each party needs the other, not as a hate object or some similar pathological reason, but as a source of satisfaction of "normal" needs'.[6]

Needing the other party as a source of satisfaction of normal needs – this is what economic interdependence and the economics of peacemaking are about.

NOTES AND REFERENCES

1. An agreed minute to Annex III to the Peace Treaty reads as follows: 'The Treaty of Peace and Annex III thereto provide for establishing normal economic relations between the parties. In accordance therewith, it is agreed that such relations will include normal commercial sales of oil by Egypt to Israel and that Israel shall be fully entitled to make bids for Egyptian-origin oil not needed for Egyptian domestic oil consumption, and Egypt and its oil concessionaires will entertain bids made by Israel, on the same basis and terms as apply to other bidders for such oil.' Agreed Minutes, pp. 2-3.

2. The president of the European Parliament stated also that trilateral cooperation between the Egyptian, Israeli and European parliaments should be encouraged.

3. See *Telex Méditerranée*, Brussels, no. 151, 20 March 1979.

4. See, for example, *Information, EEC-Egypt,* Commission of the European Community, no. 142/77.

5. See Walter Hallstein, *United Europe: Challenge and Opportunity* (Cambridge, Mass.: Harvard University Press, 1962) p. 10.

6. Rapoport, 'Threat, Trade and Love', in Martin Pfaff (ed.), *Frontiers in Social Thought: Essays in Honour of Kenneth Boulding* (Amsterdam: North-Holland, 1976) p. 272.

Selection of Equilibrium Level of Bilateral Economic Transactions

Equilibrium conditions for bilateral transactions are provided by the terms of trade and economic transactions level for which the optimal level of economic transactions chosen separately by the two countries coincide.

The objective of each country is to choose both the level of transactions T and the level of investments I_t so that expected national income E_t is maximised.

$$E_t = P_t Y_t + (1 - P_t) Y_{td} \qquad t = a,b$$

First-order conditions for maximum are:

(A.1) $\quad dE_t/dT = dC_s/dT . P_t'(C_s) C_t + P_t(C_s) \, dY_t/dT$
$$+ [1 - P_t(C_s)] \, dY_{td}/dT = 0$$

$$s = \begin{cases} b \text{ when } t = a \\ \\ a \text{ when } t = b \end{cases}$$

or

$$dE_t/dT = P_t'(C_s) C_t \, dC_s/dT + P_t(C_s) dC_t/dT - dG_{t2}/dT = 0$$

(A.2) $\quad dE_t/dI_t = -[1 - P_t(C_s)] \, dG_{t2}(I_t,T)/dI_t$
$$+ P_t(C_s) dIG_t(I_t,T)/dI_t = 0$$

or

$$dE_t/dI_t = P_t(C_s) \, dC_t/dI_t - dG_{t2}(I_t,T)/dI_t = 0$$

From equation (A.2) we get that in the optimum for $t = a,b$ and $s = b,a$:

$$p_t(C_s) \, / \, [1 \, - \, P_t(C_s)] \, = \, dG_{t2}(I_t,T)/dI_t \, / \, dIG_t(I_t,T)/dI_t$$

or

$$P_t(C_s) \, = \, dG_{t2}/dI_t \, / \, dC_t/dI_t$$

Equation (A.1) implies that for optimal level of transactions and investments $(T_t^*, \, I_t^*)$:

$$C_t \, dP_t/dT \, + \, E \, dY_t/dT \, = \, 0$$

where E is the expectation operator used on national incomes in both circumstances or, in a different form:

$$C_t \, dP_t/dT \, + \, P_t \, dC_t/dT \, = \, dG_{t2}/dT$$

at $(T_t^*, \, I_t^*)$ for t = a,b.

Equations (A.1) and (A.2) present two equations with two unknowns, T_t^* and I_t^* (optimal levels of transactions and investments, respectively, for country t).

For a given partition of gains (k), T_a^* does not have to equal T_b^*. Obviously, equilibrium requires that $T_a^* = T_b^*$. (A.1) and (A.2) provide four equations with four unknowns: $T_a^* = T_b^* = T^*$, k^*, I_a^* and I_b^*. Decisions on investment levels I_t^* (t = a,b) are obtained independently in the two countries, but the level of transactions should be equal. The shares k and (1 − k) of the two countries in the joint gains are determined, by negotiation, in such a way that equilibrium will be reached.

Parameters Estimated by the Regression Model of Border and Bilateral Trade

TABLE A.1
Border-trade Shares for Six Categories

| SITC | Ireland | | the Netherlands | | Switzerland | |
	exports	imports	exports	imports	exports	imports
00	0.5308	0.9859	0.5680	0.6355	0.9221	0.6539
01	0.2613	0.8588	0.3747	0.3086	0.5005	0.3521
02	0.4079	0.7291	0.3485	0.4891	0.7101	0.6297
03	0.3017	0.6961	0.6182	0.2716	0.5729	0.1696
04	0.7347	0.2038	0.5343	0.4325	0.5260	0.3143
05	0.7705	0.2289	0.5373	0.1860	0.3982	0.4727
06	0.6181	0.5155	0.5493	0.5123	0.4186	0.7333
07	0.8739	0.2935	0.4131	0.1326	0.3018	0.0941
08	0.9181	0.1697	0.5482	0.2406	0.4378	0.5118
09	0.2457	0.8955	0.4707	0.6462	0.2031	0.5766
11	0.6285	0.3089	0.2805	0.2233	0.2834	0.7902
12	0.0782	0.0668	0.3462	0.4398	0.1405	0.0885
21	0.7236	0.9587	0.1268	0.4804	0.7876	0.6413
22	0.9579	0.3567	0.7117	0.0217	0.6691	0.0264
23	0.4713	0.1971	0.3840	0.2234	0.7726	0.5628
24	0.9901	0.0353	0.8790	0.1579	0.9702	0.5699
25	0.9790	0.1349	0.7350	0.1354	0.9453	0.5949
26	0.7792	0.3994	0.5121	0.3098	0.7071	0.3044
27	0.2017	0.3408	0.4042	0.2663	0.9734	0.6630
28	0.1725	0.4184	0.5482	0.1492	0.7836	0.2899
29	0.7061	0.3552	0.3805	0.2502	0.6365	0.3127
32	0.6665	0.2312	0.5232	0.3823	0.5437	0.8485
33	0.9716	0.4928	0.3502	0.1389	0.7755	0.4184
34	1.0000	0.9295	0.4641	0.8435	–	–
41	0.9708	0.6423	0.7142	0.3706	0.8075	0.5362

	Ireland		the Netherlands		Switzerland	
SITC	exports	imports	exports	imports	exports	imports
42	0.8371	0.2578	0.3402	0.3440	–	–
43	0.9654	0.3413	0.4545	0.7202	0.6857	0.6827
51	0.2565	0.3543	0.3849	0.4502	0.3604	0.6092
52	1.0000	0.9511	0.3983	0.7010	0.4250	0.5166
53	0.8424	0.6008	0.3799	0.5905	0.6608	0.7061
54	0.1369	0.5878	0.4924	0.3245	0.3021	0.5867
55	0.3675	0.8202	0.4574	0.5476	0.3852	0.6347
56	0.9105	0.4745	0.1848	0.5619	0.2083	0.8205
57	0.9945	0.8765	0.5972	0.6135	0.4826	0.5144
58	0.5943	0.5330	0.2017	0.4639	0.4969	0.6115
59	0.2170	0.5162	0.2999	0.4407	0.2277	0.6212
61	0.7369	0.6193	0.5717	0.4542	0.5430	0.6945
62	0.5722	0.6557	0.6042	0.5567	0.4825	0.6919
63	0.8574	0.4444	0.6673	0.4535	0.6192	0.6552
64	0.7179	0.4767	0.6300	0.5017	0.6235	0.6259
65	0.7046	0.5494	0.5881	0.6298	0.4560	0.6273
66	0.3883	0.6974	0.5288	0.5526	0.2977	0.3737
67	0.6766	0.5412	0.4282	0.7265	0.6162	0.6629
68	0.6991	0.6959	0.4868	0.4905	0.4719	0.4052
69	0.3896	0.6805	0.4460	0.6001	0.4455	0.7927
71	0.4941	0.3980	0.3237	0.4767	0.3210	0.6903
72	0.2920	0.4315	0.3304	0.5014	0.3973	0.5979
73	0.4168	0.4920	0.3509	0.4128	0.4713	0.4237
81	0.8345	0.7382	0.6080	0.6836	0.6890	0.7516
82	0.9099	0.8078	0.7068	0.4982	0.6474	0.7984
83	0.6833	0.5714	0.6585	0.3105	0.6912	0.7891
84	0.7763	0.8235	0.7754	0.3311	0.5743	0.6287
85	0.4212	0.7251	0.8101	0.3430	0.4931	0.8218
86	0.1577	0.3610	0.3598	0.4199	0.2842	0.4848
89	0.5516	0.6431	0.5572	0.4443	0.4562	0.6420
91	0.2455	0.7935	–	–	–	–
93	0.2636	0.4263	0.4955	0.2374	–	–
94	0.5652	0.6809	–	–	0.6718	0.4550
96	0.6909	1.0000	–	–	0.7389	0.9885

TABLE A.2
Normalised Border-trade Indices

SITC	Exports				Imports				
	Ireland (1)	Netherlands (2)	Switzerland (3)	Average (1-3)	Ireland (4)	Netherlands (5)	Switzerland (6)	Average (4-6)	Overall Average (1-6)
00	0.3879	1.1469	4.6089	2.0479	2.8350	1.3367	0.6166	1.5961	1.8220
01	-0.8864	-0.4119	0.9898	-0.1028	2.1058	-0.7126	-1.2650	0.0428	-0.0300
02	-0.1914	-0.6232	2.7895	0.6583	1.3622	0.4188	0.4658	0.7489	0.7036
03	-0.6946	1.5520	1.6115	0.8229	1.1733	-0.9447	-2.4025	-0.7246	0.0492
04	1.3574	0.8751	1.2085	1.1470	-1.6497	0.0638	-1.5004	-1.0288	0.0591
05	1.5272	0.8997	0.1120	0.8463	-1.5054	-1.4813	-0.5130	-1.1666	-0.1601
06	0.8046	0.9959	0.2866	0.6957	0.1380	0.5645	1.1119	0.6048	0.6503
07	2.0173	-0.1024	-0.7155	0.3998	-1.1353	-1.8162	-2.8735	-1.9416	-0.7709
08	2.2266	0.9877	0.4515	1.2220	-1.8450	-1.1389	-0.2689	-1.0843	0.0689
09	-0.9601	0.3624	-1.5628	-0.7202	2.3166	1.4036	0.1346	1.2849	0.2824
11	0.8543	-1.1719	-0.8739	-0.3971	-1.0470	-1.2475	1.4666	-0.2759	-0.3365
12	-1.7538	-0.6412	-2.1001	-1.4983	-2.4346	0.1099	-2.9084	-1.7444	-1.6214
21	1.3047	-2.4115	3.4542	0.7825	2.6791	0.3643	0.5383	1.1939	0.9882
22	2.4151	2.3059	1.4371	2.3860	-0.7729	-2.5110	-3.2953	-2.1930	0.0965
23	0.1089	-0.3367	3.3256	1.0326	-1.6878	-1.2468	0.0485	0.9620	0.0353
24	2.5678	3.6553	5.9219	3.7483	-2.6159	-1.6575	0.0931	-1.3935	1.1774
25	2.5150	2.4940	4.8078	3.2723	-2.0448	-1.7983	0.2487	-1.1981	1.0371
26	1.5683	0.6965	2.7630	1.6759	-0.5278	-0.7053	-1.5622	-0.9318	0.3721
27	-1.1686	-0.1742	5.0491	1.2354	-0.8638	-0.9781	0.6733	-0.3895	0.4230
28	-1.3070	0.9869	3.4198	1.0332	-0.4188	-1.7119	-1.6529	-1.2612	-0.1140
29	1.2219	-0.3654	2.1571	1.0045	-0.7814	-1.0789	-1.5106	-1.1236	-0.0596
32	1.0339	0.7856	1.3619	0.0605	-1.4924	-0.2506	1.8299	0.0290	0.5447
33	2.4800	-0.6096	3.3499	0.7401	0.0074	-1.7769	-0.8518	-0.8738	0.4332
34	2.6147	0.3085	—	1.4616	2.5118	1.6405	-0.1171	2.5762	2.0189
41	2.4763	2.3256	3.6249	2.8089	-1.3400	-0.3241	—	0.1412	1.4751
42	1.8427	-0.6897	2.5794	0.5765	-0.8614	-0.4908	0.7971	-0.9154	-0.1695
43	2.4506	0.2315	-0.2134	1.7538	-0.7869	1.8675	0.3376	0.6011	1.1775
51	-0.9091	-0.3303	-0.2134	-0.4843	2.6352	0.1748	-0.2392	-0.0915	-0.2879
52	2.6147	-0.2216	0.3413	0.9155	0.6266	1.7474	0.9421	1.3811	1.1463
53	1.8677	-0.3702	2.3658	1.2878	0.5524	1.0546	0.9421	0.8744	1.0811
54	-1.4759	0.5369	-0.7133	-0.5508	0.5524	-0.6129	0.1980	0.0458	-0.2525

SITC	Exports				Imports				Overall Average (1-6)
	Ireland (1)	Netherlands (2)	Switzerland (3)	Average (1-3)	Ireland (4)	Netherlands (5)	Switzerland (6)	Average (4-6)	
55	-0.3827	0.2553	0.0002	-0.0524	1.8847	0.7855	0.4971	0.1557	0.5067
56	2.1905	-1.9434	-1.5179	-0.4236	-0.0974	0.8753	1.6553	0.8111	0.1937
57	2.5885	1.3824	0.8364	1.0624	2.2078	1.1981	-0.2528	1.0510	1.3267
58	0.6915	-1.8067	0.9590	-0.0520	0.2380	0.2612	0.3525	0.2839	0.1159
59	-1.0964	-1.0151	-1.3518	-1.1544	0.1419	0.1152	0.4128	0.2233	-0.4656
61	1.3679	1.1766	1.3547	1.2997	0.7330	0.1998	0.8695	0.6008	0.9503
62	0.5873	1.4386	0.8354	0.9538	0.9414	0.8429	0.8537	0.8793	0.9165
63	1.9388	1.9474	2.0088	1.9650	-0.2702	0.1959	0.6246	0.1834	1.0742
64	1.2778	1.6470	2.0459	1.6569	-0.0849	0.4981	0.4423	0.2851	0.9710
65	1.2147	1.3092	0.6077	1.0439	0.3319	1.3011	0.4511	0.6947	0.8693
66	-0.2845	0.8305	-0.7514	-0.0685	1.1809	0.8168	-1.1301	0.2892	0.1104
67	1.0819	0.0191	1.9832	1.0281	0.2851	1.9073	0.6728	0.9550	0.9916
68	1.1887	0.4918	0.7440	0.8082	1.1722	0.4275	-0.9341	0.2218	0.5150
69	-0.2782	0.1631	0.5174	0.1341	1.0836	1.1150	1.4816	1.2267	0.6804
71	0.2169	-0.8230	-0.5514	-0.3858	-0.5360	0.3414	0.8467	0.2174	-0.0842
72	-0.7408	-0.7694	0.1040	-0.4688	-0.3439	0.4963	0.2673	0.1399	-0.1644
73	-0.1491	-0.6033	0.7390	-0.0045	0.0031	-0.0592	-0.8188	-0.2916	-0.1480
81	1.8306	1.4692	2.6078	1.9692	1.4147	1.6384	1.2255	1.4262	1.6977
82	2.1881	2.2662	2.2504	2.2349	1.8136	0.4760	1.5177	1.2691	1.7520
83	1.1138	1.8767	2.6263	1.8723	0.4583	-0.7012	1.4593	0.5055	1.1389
84	1.5548	2.8196	1.6235	1.9993	1.9029	-0.5720	0.4594	0.5971	1.2982
85	-0.1283	3.0989	0.9267	1.2991	1.3397	-0.4972	1.6634	0.8353	1.0672
86	-1.3773	-0.5324	-0.8670	-0.9256	-0.7482	-0.0153	-0.4437	-0.4024	-0.6640
89	0.4895	1.0594	0.6095	0.7195	0.8695	0.1383	0.5422	0.5167	0.6181
91	-0.9613	-	-	-0.9613	1.7316	-	-	1.7316	-0.9613
93	-0.8752	0.5624	-	-0.1564	-0.3739	-1.1590	-	-0.7665	-0.4614
94	0.5541	-	2.4603	1.5072	1.0857	-	-0.6231	0.2313	0.8693
96	1.1498	-	3.0357	2.0928	2.9157	-	2.7025	2.8091	2.4509

Note: for derivation of indices see text.

TABLE A.3
Border-trade Indices

SITC	Border-trade index	SITC	Border-trade index
12	–1.6214	55	0.5067
91	–0.9613	68	0.5150
07	–0.7709	32	0.5447
86	–0.6640	89	0.6181
59	–0.4656	06	0.6503
93	–0.4614	69	0.6804
11	–0.3365	02	0.7036
51	–0.2879	94	0.8693
54	–0.2525	65	0.8693
42	–0.1695	62	0.9165
72	–0.1644	61	0.9503
05	–0.1601	64	0.9710
73	–0.1480	21	0.9882
28	–0.1140	67	0.9916
71	–0.0842	25	1.0371
29	–0.0596	85	1.0672
01	–0.0300	63	1.0742
23	0.0353	53	1.0811
03	0.0492	83	1.1389
04	0.0591	52	1.1463
08	0.0689	24	1.0774
22	0.0965	43	1.1775
66	0.1104	84	1.2982
58	0.1159	57	1.3267
56	0.1937	41	1.4751
09	0.2824	81	1.6977
26	0.3721	82	1.7520
27	0.4230	00	1.8220
33	0.4332	34	2.0189
		96	2.4509

TABLE A.4
Summary of Results of Regression Parameters

SITC	GNP(i)		GNP(i)		DGNP(ij)		DIST(ij)		$TM_A(ij)$		$TX_A(ij)$		CONSTANT		R^2	$Adj\ R^2_i$	F	n	$RES_M(ij)^a$
	C	T	C	T	C	T	C	T	C	T	C	T	C	T					
00	0.50	3.84	0.38	3.00	—	—	-0.89	-6.19	0.68	5.37	0.63	6.63	-5.23	-4.55	0.41	0.40	31.77	231	—
01	—	—	—	—	—	—	-0.64	-5.14	1.00	7.84	1.28	8.24	-6.57	-5.61	0.39	0.34	51.58	242	—
02	0.35	3.03	—	—	-0.20	-1.78	-0.38	-3.07	0.63	4.95	0.71	13.09	-3.37	-3.87	0.59	0.58	67.59	239	-0.25
03	0.19	2.02	—	—	—	—	-0.85	-9.93	0.93	8.16	1.25	15.80	-5.90	-9.84	0.59	0.58	90.93	256	—
04	0.12	1.75	0.40	5.08	0.15	2.13	-0.49	-6.56	1.46	14.63	1.06	14.31	-11.56	-16.24	0.73	0.72	136.79	258	—
05	—	—	0.43	5.62	0.20	2.41	-0.54	-7.73	0.86	10.70	1.12	14.05	-8.17	-12.35	0.72	0.71	131.10	260	-0.64
06	0.37	4.10	0.25	3.31	0.16	1.90	-0.68	-7.77	0.58	4.18	0.98	9.16	-6.26	-7.04	0.48	0.47	39.32	259	-0.81
07	0.48	6.00	0.43	5.67	—	—	-0.65	-7.08	0.51	6.98	1.39	22.28	-9.96	-13.68	0.74	0.74	122.26	255	-0.75
08	0.23	2.44	0.38	3.52	—	—	-0.48	-4.24	1.45	8.50	1.35	10.37	-13.14	-10.19	0.55	0.54	62.89	257	—
09	0.51	6.70	0.24	3.36	—	—	-0.64	-7.59	0.87	6.46	0.80	10.48	-6.79	-7.72	0.56	0.56	65.51	254	—
11	0.18	1.74	0.27	3.40	—	—	-0.50	-5.09	1.24	6.88	1.16	14.00	-9.89	-9.98	0.63	0.62	87.05	259	—
12	—	—	—	—	—	—	—	—	0.97	7.89	1.20	13.23	-7.88	-9.69	0.48	0.48	115.28	247	0.00
21	—	—	—	—	0.37	-3.30	-0.23	-2.12	1.06	10.05	1.04	7.64	-5.25	-5.38	0.44	0.43	45.42	236	—
22	—	—	—	—	—	—	-0.27	-2.18	0.92	9.05	0.86	13.47	-4.75	-6.77	0.54	0.54	88.78	225	—
23	0.39	3.64	0.33	2.38	—	—	-0.60	-7.80	0.63	4.30	1.08	24.96	-5.07	-8.97	0.75	0.75	182.68	242	—
24	—	—	—	—	—	—	-0.52	-4.65	0.86	6.78	1.02	9.89	-6.62	-6.90	0.57	0.56	80.03	243	—
25	-0.34	-1.83	0.29	3.26	—	—	-0.53	-3.89	0.93	4.68	1.05	14.13	-2.99	-3.49	0.55	0.54	61.93	205	—
26	0.16	1.96	—	—	—	—	-0.57	0.07	0.86	9.02	1.05	14.71	-7.14	-12.73	0.75	0.74	151.91	255	—
27	0.31	3.83	—	—	—	—	-0.64	-9.01	0.88	7.96	1.64	16.91	-9.27	-13.25	0.66	0.66	126.60	259	—
28	—	—	—	—	—	—	-0.67	-7.41	0.96	18.36	1.34	14.24	-6.54	-11.23	0.69	0.69	185.85	246	—
29	0.33	4.97	0.26	4.40	—	—	-0.53	-9.03	0.72	9.37	0.97	11.26	-6.50	-12.80	0.72	0.71	131.37	258	—
32	—	—	0.69	4.03	—	—	-0.65	-4.21	0.72	4.11	0.85	7.85	-6.17	-4.86	0.50	0.49	47.88	194	—
33	0.52	6.29	0.25	2.50	0.26	2.84	-0.84	-8.37	0.61	5.75	1.69	16.03	-11.83	-12.01	0.71	0.70	99.41	250	-1.01
34	—	—	-1.28	-5.70	—	—	-0.76	-4.64	0.73	7.48	1.42	8.62	2.21	2.20	0.52	0.51	42.85	161	—
41	—	—	0.44	3.88	0.31	2.96	-0.39	-3.34	0.36	3.90	0.58	7.71	-2.39	-3.07	0.35	0.34	36.45	202	—
42	0.24	2.02	—	—	—	—	-0.32	-3.19	1.10	8.67	1.09	13.44	-7.83	-9.09	0.51	0.50	63.28	244	-0.12
43	0.24	3.10	—	—	-0.22	-3.42	-0.52	-4.02	0.90	4.23	0.78	7.52	-4.19	-3.40	0.39	0.38	35.41	222	—
51	—	—	—	—	—	—	-0.32	-4.78	0.89	7.14	1.10	17.71	-6.84	-8.71	0.68	0.68	111.69	260	-0.18
52	—	—	—	—	—	—	-0.50	-3.50	0.78	5.28	0.47	5.94	-0.81	-0.89	0.32	0.31	26.78	168	—
53	0.45	4.39	0.30	4.41	-0.17	-2.47	-0.50	-6.32	0.57	3.20	0.86	19.71	-5.57	-7.38	0.78	0.77	146.53	252	-0.39
54	0.15	2.26	—	—	-0.11	-1.70	-0.20	-2.97	0.88	6.83	1.10	17.94	-6.59	-8.59	0.66	0.66	100.60	257	-0.13
55	0.57	6.79	-0.31	4.44	—	—	-0.69	-8.59	0.97	5.39	1.00	12.85	-9.10	-9.90	0.71	0.71	127.70	258	—

SITC	GNP(ij) C	GNP(ij) T	GNP(i) C	GNP(i) T	DGNP(ij) C	DGNP(ij) T	DIST(ij) C	DIST(ij) T	$TM_h(i)$ C	$TM_h(i)$ T	$TX_h(i)$ C	$TX_h(i)$ T	CONSTANT C	CONSTANT T	R^2	Adj. R^2	F	n	$RES_h(ij)$[a]
56	0.20	1.80	–	–	–	–	-0.48	-3.90	1.17	4.45	0.79	7.67	-4.91	-3.27	0.31	0.30	32.53	219	–
57	0.17	3.00	–	–	–	–	-0.57	-5.27	0.87	5.24	0.42	10.74	-1.85	-2.47	0.50	0.49	48.10	191	–
58	0.30	4.19	0.42	6.47	–	–	-0.59	-8.37	0.93	11.88	0.75	22.25	-6.51	-10.52	0.82	0.81	226.49	253	–
59	0.38	4.00	0.15	2.86	-0.15	-2.80	-0.48	-7.75	1.02	8.12	0.87	22.85	-6.75	-10.94	0.82	0.82	198.44	258	-0.39
61	0.52	6.88	0.33	3.92	–	–	-0.58	-7.37	0.77	5.67	1.07	10.25	-7.82	-11.44	0.67	0.66	104.60	258	–
62	0.26	3.28	0.34	5.96	–	–	-0.67	-10.63	0.32	2.35	0.87	20.41	-4.90	-7.42	0.79	0.79	196.13	257	–
63	0.41	5.54	0.62	6.71	–	–	-0.63	-8.19	0.71	6.23	0.67	5.86	-6.26	-8.77	0.61	0.61	82.08	258	–
64	0.30	5.14	0.52	7.83	-0.17	-2.54	-0.66	-8.38	0.71	4.60	0.74	17.96	-6.38	-7.09	0.77	0.76	138.79	254	-0.55
65	0.39	4.83	0.47	8.50	0.09	1.94	-0.62	-10.37	0.71	6.17	0.76	12.49	-6.80	-9.44	0.76	0.76	138.76	260	-0.68
66	0.29	2.79	0.19	2.31	–	–	-0.51	-6.83	1.03	8.41	1.20	10.90	-10.15	-13.06	0.71	0.71	130.36	260	–
67	0.47	4.87	0.47	5.55	–	–	-0.72	-9.02	0.89	5.71	0.92	14.92	-8.23	-10.82	0.77	0.77	177.29	257	–
68	0.34	5.77	0.32	3.51	–	–	-0.70	-9.67	0.81	6.64	1.16	12.97	-9.18	-15.12	0.78	0.78	187.01	258	–
69	0.27	3.92	0.35	7.31	–	–	-0.58	-11.48	1.03	9.55	0.85	24.83	-8.52	-15.29	0.86	0.85	315.64	260	–
71	0.33	4.34	0.21	4.39	–	–	-0.48	-9.46	1.07	8.72	0.97	26.68	-9.29	-14.43	0.86	0.86	322.72	259	–
72	0.19	3.11	0.25	4.32	–	–	-0.60	-10.46	0.92	6.67	0.97	21.29	-8.26	-11.66	0.81	0.80	218.91	259	–
73	0.67	8.43	0.52	7.20	–	–	-0.64	-9.28	1.33	12.78	0.89	15.65	-10.91	-15.93	0.79	0.79	200.40	259	–
81	0.46	5.92	0.65	8.33	–	–	-0.90	-9.96	0.29	2.24	0.68	13.53	-5.56	-6.98	0.70	0.70	121.13	255	–
82	0.26	3.56	0.60	7.90	–	–	-0.69	-7.20	0.66	6.63	0.78	13.66	-7.35	-10.15	0.74	0.74	140.02	241	–
83	0.36	5.08	0.22	2.45	–	–	-0.54	-7.26	0.74	10.33	1.02	13.30	-5.94	-11.43	0.72	0.72	131.54	252	–
84	0.45	5.53	0.58	7.48	0.14	2.04	-0.74	-9.44	0.83	8.91	0.98	10.64	-9.46	-12.96	0.73	0.73	118.01	260	-0.83
85	0.33	5.10	0.53	6.37	–	–	-0.56	-6.41	0.72	8.13	1.17	15.08	-9.72	-14.12	0.72	0.72	130.00	247	–
86	0.37	5.57	0.17	3.88	-0.16	-3.69	-0.41	-8.55	0.73	7.70	1.03	34.32	-6.67	-14.86	0.90	0.89	380.48	260	-0.31
89	–	–	0.36	6.98	-0.08	1.83	-0.53	-10.29	0.89	10.14	0.94	19.87	-8.31	-15.92	0.84	0.84	231.06	260	-0.48
91	0.30	2.46	0.29	2.04	-0.30	-1.92	-0.97	-6.09	1.49	12.96	1.12	8.12	-5.80	-5.58	0.74	0.72	50.28	93	-0.78
93	0.30	2.46	0.51	3.20	0.40	3.07	-0.63	-4.55	1.18	11.89	0.76	3.67	-10.32	-9.28	0.58	0.57	44.35	192	-0.88
94	0.27	2.74	0.14	1.64	–	–	-0.53	-5.51	0.59	6.82	1.00	9.29	-4.01	-6.13	0.49	0.48	51.71	214	–

[a] When not listed, $RES_h(ij)$ equals the coefficient of DIST(ij)

C = Coefficient

T = t values

Text of the Egyptian-Israeli Agreement on Trade and Commerce

Set out below is the text of the Egyptian-Israeli agreement on trade and commerce signed on 8 May 1980.

AGREEMENT ON TRADE AND COMMERCE BETWEEN THE STATE OF ISRAEL AND THE ARAB REPUBLIC OF EGYPT

Desiring to normalize relations between their two countries in accordance with the Treaty of Peace done in Washington, D.C. on the 26th of March 1979, and in pursuance of Article III thereof, and Annex III Article 2 thereof.

Desiring to encourage trade relations between the two countries, and to promote such relations on the basis of equality and mutual advantage.

The Government of the State of Israel, and the Government of the Arab Republic of Egypt,

Have agreed as follows:

Article I:
To ensure the free movement of goods between the two countries, each party will make available to the other party, laws, regulations and procedures prevailing in his country, concerning the importation and exportation of goods and commodities, customs tariffs and other duties and excise, as well as any amendments or alterations thereto.

Article II:
The exchange of goods and commodities between the two countries shall be effected in accordance with the laws, rules, regulations governing import and export regime in each country.

The parties, subject to their laws and regulations, and when so required, shall grant import licenses after an application is made by the importer to the competent authorities in either country.

Article III:

A) Both parties shall act in their mutual trade relations, in accordance with all the rights, duties and privileges determined in the international Conventions to which they both adhered.

B) Both parties shall accord to each other Most Favoured Nation Treatment.

In accordance with Article 24 of the General Agreement on Tariffs and Trade, the provisions of Article III of this Agreement relating to the Most Favoured Nation Treatment shall not apply to the following:

1) Preferences and advantages accorded to the Arab countries by the Arab Republic of Egypt.

2) Preferences and advantages which result from any customs union or free trade area to which either of the two parties is or may become a party.

3) Preferences and advantages resulting from multilateral arrangements aiming to establish or accomplish any form of integration, to which either of the two parties is or may become a party.

Article IV:

In accordance with its laws, regulations, and trade practice with the other countries, either party may require that a certificate of origin is to be issued and authenticated by the competent authorities designated for such, in connection with the goods and commodities imported from the other party.

If so decided, the exporting party has to comply with such.

Article V:

Each party shall comply with the other's quarantine, phytosanitary, veterinary and health regulations and shall recognize the certificates issued by the relevant authorities in respect of agricultural products fresh and processed, as well as animals, products of animal origin, biological products, and products for animal feeding.

Such certificates shall be issued in accordance with the requirements of the importing country and with the international regulations, and signed by the authorized officials.

Article VI:

In order to enhance the performance of trade relations, each party, in accordance with its prevailing laws and regulations, shall permit and facilitate in its country the setting up by the other party of trade centres, participation in exhibitions and fairs, and visits of trade delegations, and will facilitate according to the normal practice the access of samples and goods destined for exhibitions and fairs.

Article VII:
Payments between the two countries shall be effected in any convertible currency, in accordance with the prevailing exchange laws and currency regulations in each country.

Article VIII:
In order to facilitate and to follow up the implementation of this agreement, a joint committee composed of representatives of both parties shall be established, and shall meet once a year or whenever agreed by the two parties, alternately in each country.

Article IX:
The task of this joint committee shall be:–
A) To review the administration of this agreement.
B) To review the progress of trade and the flow of goods and commodities between the two countries.
C) To consult and to solve problems which may derive from putting this agreement into practice.
D) To co-ordinate the transfer of information agreed upon.
E) To review any matter that may be raised by either party.

Article X:
This agreement is subject to the necessary requirements and procedures of ratification in each country, and shall enter into force upon exchanging instruments of ratification between the two countries.

Article XI:
This agreement shall be valid for one year starting from the date it enters into force, and shall be extended automatically for equivalent periods of one year each, unless either of the two parties notifies the other of its intention to terminate it, before three months prior to the expiry of each yearly period.

Done and signed in Cairo, on May 8, 1980, in two originals in each of the Hebrew, Arabic and English languages, all the three texts being equally authentic.

In case of divergent interpretation, the English text shall prevail.

Selected Bibliography

AGARWAL, JAMUNA P., 'Determinants of Foreign Direct Investment: a Survey', *Weltwirtschaftliches Archiv*, Kiel, vol. 116, no. 4, 1980, pp. 739-73.

ARAD, RUTH, and SEEV HIRSCH, 'Determinants of Trade Flows and Choice of Trade Patterns: Reconciling the Heckscher-Ohlin and Linder Models of International Trade', *Weltwirtschaftliches Archiv*, Kiel, vol. 117, no. 2, 1981, pp. 276-97.

ARON, RAYMOND, *The Century of Total War* (Boston: Beacon Press, 1966).

ARROW, KENNETH J., *Social Choice and Individual Values* (New Haven and London: Yale University Press, 1951).

ASKARI, H., and V. CORB, 'Economic Implications of Military Expenditures in the Middle East', *Journal of Peace Research*, Oslo, vol. XI, no. 4, 1974.

BALASSA, BELA, *Theory of Economic Integration* (Homewood, Illinois: Richard Irwin, 1962).

BERGLAS, EYTAN, 'Preferential Trading Theory: the n Commodity Case', *Journal of Political Economy*, Chicago, April 1979, pp. 315-31.

BLACKHURST, RICHARD, NICOLAS MARIAN and JAN TUMLIR, *Trade Liberalization, Protectionism and Interdependence*, GATT Studies in International Trade No. 5 (Geneva: GATT Secretariat, 1977).

BOHRER, H., 'Die deutsch-französichen Wirtschaftsbeziehungen und die Möglichkeiten ihrer zukunftigen Gestaltung', *Europa-Archiv*, Viertes Jahr, July-December 1949.

BOULDING, KENNETH E., 'The Relation of Economic, Political and Social Systems', *Social and Economic Studies*, Mona, Jamaica, December 1962, pp. 351-62, republished in Boulding, *Towards a General Social Science, Collected Papers, Volume 4* (Boulder, Colorado: Colorado Associated University Press, 1974) pp. 148-62.

BOULDING, KENNETH E., *The Economics of Love and Fear: a Preface to Grants Economics* (Belmont, California: Wadsworth, 1973).

BREWSTER, HAVELOCK R., 'Economic Dependence: a Quantitative Interpretation', *Social and Economic Studies*, Mona, Jamaica, March 1973.

BROWN, LESTER R., *World Without Borders* (New York: Random House, 1972).

BRUTON, HENRY J., *The Promise of Peace: Economic Cooperation between Egypt and Israel*, Staff Paper (Washington: Brookings Institution, 1980).

BUCKLEY, PETER, and MARK CASSON, *The Future of the Multinational Enterprise* (New York: Holmes & Meier, 1979).

CAPORASO, JAMES A., 'Introduction', *International Organization*, Boston, Special Issue, Winter 1978, pp. 1-12.

CAPORASO, JAMES A., 'Dependence, Dependency, and Power in the Global System: a Structural and Behavioral Analysis', *International Organization*, Boston, Winter 1978, pp. 13-43.

CARDOSO, FERNANDO H., 'Associated Development', in A. Stepan (ed.), *Authoritarian Brazil: Policies and Futures* (New Haven: Yale University Press, 1973).

CARR, E. H., *The Twenty Years' Crisis, 1919-1939*, 2nd ed. (New York: Harper & Row, 1964) (first edition published in 1939).

CARR, E. H., *The Future of Nations: Independence or Interdependence* (London: Kegan Paul, 1941).

CASSON, MARK *Alternatives to the Multinational Enterprise* (London: Macmillan, 1979).

COOPER, RICHARD N., *The Economics of Interdependence: Economic Policy in the Atlantic Community* (New York: McGraw-Hill, for the Council on Foreign Relations, 1968).

COOPER, RICHARD N., 'Trade Policy is Foreign Policy', *Foreign Policy*, New York, Winter 1972-73.

CORBET, HUGH, 'One Course of Recovery for an Ailing European Community', *The World Economy*, London, March 1981, pp. 57-68.

CORDEN, W. M., 'Economies of Scale and Customs Union Theory', *Journal of Political Economy*, Chicago, 1972, pp. 465-75.

DIEBOLD, WILLIAM Jr, *The Schuman Plan* (New York: Praeger, 1959).

DOS SANTOS, TH., 'The Structure of Dependence', *American Economic Review*, Papers and Proceedings of the American Economic Association, May 1970.

DUNNING, JOHN H., 'Explaining Changing Patterns of International Production: in Defence of the Eclectic Theory', in Sanjaya Lall (guest editor), *Oxford Bulletin of Economics and Statistics*, Oxford, Special Issue, November 1979.

DUNNING, JOHN H., 'Trade, Location of Economic Activity and the Multinational Enterprise: a Search for an Eclectic Approach', in Bertil Ohlin, Per-Ove Hesselborn and Per Magnus Wijkman (eds), *The International Allocation of Economic Activity* (London: Macmillan, 1977).

DUVALL, RAYMOND D., 'Dependence and Dependencia Theory: Notes Towards Precision of Concept and Argument', *International Organization*, Boston, Winter 1978, pp. 51-78.

FEIGE, EDGAR, 'The Economic Consequences of Peace in the Middle East', *Challenge*, New York, January-February 1979.

GALTUNG, JOHAN, entry on 'Peace' in the *International Encyclopedia of the Social Sciences* (London: Macmillan, 1968; and New York: the Free Press, 1968) vol. 11.

GROSSER, ALFRED, *Les Occidentaux* (Paris: Fayard, 1978).

HALLSTEIN, WALTER, *United Europe: Challenge and Opportunity* (Cambridge, Mass.: Harvard University Press, 1962).

HAZLEWOOD, ARTHUR, *Economic Integration: The East African Experience*.(New York: St Martin's Press, 1975).

HIRSCH, SEEV, 'Hypotheses Regarding the Trade between Developing and Industrialized Countries', in Herbert Giersch (ed.), *The International Division of Labour; Problems and Prospects* (Tübingen: J.C.B. Mohr, for the Institut für Weltwirtschaft an der Universität Kiel, 1974).

HIRSCH, SEEV, 'An International Trade and Investment Theory of the Firm', *Oxford Economic Papers*, Oxford, July 1976, pp. 258-70.

HIRSCHMAN, ALBERT O., *National Power and the Structure of Foreign Trade* (Berkeley: University of California Press, 1945).

HIRSCHMAN, ALBERT O., *How to Divest in Latin America and Why*, Essays in International Finance No. 76 (Princeton: Princeton University Press, 1969).

HIRSCHMAN, ALBERT O., 'Beyond Asymmetry: Critical Notes on Myself as a Young Man and on Some Other Old Friends', *International Organization*, Boston, Winter, pp. 45-50.

JACKSON, JOHN H., *World Trade and the Law of GATT* (New York: McGraw-Hill, 1969).

JOHNSON, HARRY G., 'A Theoretical Model of Economic Nationalism in New Developing States', *Political Quarterly*, Toronto, June 1965.

JOHNSON, HARRY G., 'An Economic Theory of Protectionism, Tariff Bargaining, and the Formation of Customs Unions', *Journal of Political Economy*, Chicago, June 1965.

JONES, KENT, 'Forgetfulness of Things Past: Europe and the Steel Cartel', *The World Economy*, London, May 1979.

KEESING, DONALD B., and MARTIN WOLF, *Textile Quotas against Developing Countries,* Thames Essay No. 23 (London: Trade Policy Research Centre, 1980).

KEOHANE, ROBERT O. and JOSEPH S. NYE, *Power and Interdependence* (Boston: Little, Brown, 1977).

KEY, VLADIMIR O. Jr, *Politics, Parties and Pressure Groups*, 4th ed. (New York: Crowell, 1958).

KEYNES, JOHN MAYNARD, *The Economic Consequences of the Peace*, reprinted edition (London: Macmillan, 1971; and New York: St Martin's Press, 1971) (first edition printed in 1921).

KINDLEBERGER, CHARLES P., *American Business Abroad* (New Haven: Yale University Press, 1969).

KRAUSS, MELVYN B., 'Recent Developments in Customs Union Theory: an Interpretative Survey', *Journal of Economic Literature*, Nashville, Tennessee, June 1972.

LALL, SANJAYA, 'Is "Dependence" a Useful Concept in Analyzing Underdevelopment?', *World Development*, Oxford, November-December 1975.

L'HUILLIER, JACQUES, *Théorie et Pratique de la Coopération Économique International* (Paris: Génin, 1975).

LINDER, STAFFAN BURENSTAM, *An Essay on Trade and Transformation* (New York: John Wiley, 1961).

LINNEMANN, HANS, *An Econometric Study of International Trade Flows* (Amsterdam: North-Holland, 1966).

LIPSEY, RICHARD G., 'The Theory of Customs Unions: a General Survey', *Economic Journal*, London, September 1960.

MACHLUP, FRITZ, *A History of Thought on Economic Integration* (London: Macmillan, for the International Economics Association, 1977).

MEADE, JAMES E., *The Theory of Customs Unions* (Amsterdam: North-Holland, 1955).

MERLE, MARCEL (ed.), *Pacifisme et Internationalisme* (Paris: Armand Colin, 1966).

MORGENTHAU, HANS J., *Politics Among Nations: The Struggle for Power and Peace*, 5th ed. (New York: A.A. Knopf, 1973).

MORGENTHAU, HANS J., 'The New Diplomacy of Movement', *Encounter*, London, August 1974.

OHLIN, BERTIL, PER-OVE HESSELBORN and PER MAGNUS WIJKMAN (eds), *The International Allocation of Economic Activity* (London: Macmillan, 1977).

OLSON, MANCUR Jr, *The Logic of Collective Action: Public Goods and the Theory of Groups* (Cambridge, Mass.: Harvard University Press, 1965).

RAPOPORT, ANATOL, 'Prisoner's Dilemma: Recollections and Observations', in Anatol Rapoport (ed.), *Game Theory as a Theory of Conflict* (Dordrecht, Holland: Reidel, 1974).

RAPOPORT, ANATOL, 'Threat, Trade and Love', in Martin Pfaff (ed.), *Frontiers in Social Thought: Essays in Honour of Kenneth Boulding* (Amsterdam: North-Holland, 1976).

ROBSON, PETER, 'The New Setting for Economic Cooperation in East Africa', in Peter Robson (ed.), *International Economic Integration* (Harmondsworth: Penguin Books, 1972).

SILBERNER, EDMUND (ed.), *La Guerre et la Paix dans l'Histoire des Doctrines Économiques* (Paris: Sirey, 1957).

SNYDER, GLENN H., *Deterrence and Defence* (Princeton: Princeton University Press, 1961).

SOWDEN, J. K., *The German Question, 1945-1973* (New York: St Martin's Press, 1975).

TOVIAS, ALFRED, *Tariff Preferences in Mediterranean Diplomacy* (London: Macmillan, for the Trade Policy Research Centre, 1977).

TOVIAS, ALFRED, *Théorie et Pratique des Accords Commerciaux Préférentiels* (Bern: Herbert Lang, 1974).

VINER, JACOB, *The Customs Union Issue* (New York: Carnegie Endowment for International Peace, 1950).

WALL, DAVID, 'Export Processing Zones', *Journal of World Trade Law*, Twickenham, United Kingdom, September-October 1976.

WALTZ, KENNETH N., 'The Myth of National Interdependence', in Charles P. Kindleberger (ed.), *The International Corporation* (Cambridge, Mass.: MIT Press, 1970).

WILSON, J. A., 'The Policies of Regulation' in J. W. McKie (ed.), *Social Responsibility and the Business Predicament* (Washington: Brookings Institution, 1974).

YEATS, ALEXANDER J., 'Tariff Valuation, Transport Costs and Establishment of Trade Preferences among Developing Countries', *World Development*, Oxford, February 1980.

Index

Acheson, Dean, 127
Africa, 133, 142
Agreement on Trade and
    Commerce, Egyptian-Israeli,
    139, 157
American, 12, 136
Arab boycott, 121, 137
Arab-Israeli conflict, 117, 136
Austria, 89
autonomy, 10, 14-17
Autonomy, 87, 135

balance
    of prosperity, 4-7
    of terror, 4-7, 34
Balkans, 19, 48
Begin, Menachem, 3
Belgium, 89, 127
belligerency, 3, 4, 53
bilateral
    cooperation, 76, 122, 128
    relations, 19, 23, 135
    trade, 50, 81, 94, 105, 113, 115,
        118, 121, 124, 135, 140
    transactions, 7-9, 24, 26-9, 33,
        36-43, 47, 51, 65, 67, 71, 79,
        118, 136-7, 144
    ventures, 76, 79-80
border trade, 8, 88-94, 105-6, 122
Boulding, Kenneth E., 3-4, 145
Brown, Lester R., 12

CACM (Central American
    Common Market), 13
Caporaso, James A., 15-18
Cardoso, Fernando H., 18
Caribbean, 12, 142
Carr, E.H., 11, 13
Comecon (Council for Mutual
    . Economic Assistance), 13
common market, 120, 132
consumer interests, 50
Cooper, Richard N., 10, 20
cooperative venture, 71-4, 76-81, 82
cost
    of adjustment, 95
    of dissociation, 26-44, 61-4, 143-4
    transfer, 9, 26, 52-3, 56, 64, 71,
        82, 88-9, 94-5, 103-5, 106, 138,
        140
    of transportation, 9, 52, 66
customs union, 120, 124-6

dependence, 6, 10, 12-20, 23-6,
    28-34, 36, 43-4, 64, 67, 117, 139,
    143-4
dependencia, 16-19
dependency, 10, 15-19
deterrence, 12, 34-7
direct investment, 8, 71, 73-4, 138
dissociation, 26-8, 33-4, 37-9, 41-2,
    62, 79-81, 143-5
distance

cultural, 53
economic, 95-7, 102-3, 112, 114
geographical, 94-7, 100, 112, 114
physical, 53, 97, 102-3
dominance, 14, 17-18, 74-5, 78-9,
  81, 82
Dunning, John J., 73

East-West, 11, 87
economies of scale, 7-9, 26, 52, 62,
  66-7, 82, 103, 125-7
ECSC (European Coal and Steel
  Community), 126-8, 144-5
EFTA ((European Free Trade
  Association), 142
Egypt, 3, 5, 43, 44, 66-7, 87, 88, 89,
  94-7, 101, 103-15, 117-19, 121-6,
  128-32, 135-43
Eilat, 123
El Arish, 123
Europe, 10-12, 89, 105, 119, 126-8,
  136
European Community, 13, 15, 101,
  124-6, 128, 131, 140, 142-3
exchange system, see system
export
  creation, 53, 59-64, 67, 71, 79, 81,
    88, 103, 138
  diversion, 53-6, 60-3, 71, 88, 103,
    105
  expansion, 53, 56-63, 88, 103
  processing zones, 122, 123

France, 89, 126-8, 144
free trade area, 51, 122–4, 127, 129,
  142
free trade zone, see free trade area

Galtung, Johan, 8
game theory, 4, 37

GATT (General Agreement on
  Tariffs and Trade), 118-24, 143
Germany, 3, 8, 19, 48, 89, 126-8,
  144
Greece, 143

Heckscher-Ohlin Model, 95-7
Hirschman, Albert O., 19, 20, 23,
  24, 48

import expansion, 53, 56-63, 88, 103
independence, 23, 25, 32, 36
integration theory, 51, 53, 88
integrative system, see system
interdependence, 3, 8, 10-17, 20,
  23, 28-37, 43-5, 47, 143-5
  sensitivity, 14
  vulnerability, 14
Ireland, 89-91
irrevocable
  dependence, 32, 44
  interdependence, 32-3, 36, 145
Israel, 44, 45, 66-7, 87-9, 94-7, 101,
  103-15, 117-19, 121-5, 128-32,
  135-43
Italy, 89, 127, 143

Japan, 7, 14, 131, 136
Jerusalem, 5
Johnson, Harry G., 124
joint ventures, 47, 64, 138

Keohane, Robert O., 12-14
Key, Vladimir O., 50
Keynes, John Maynard, 3
Kindleberger, Charles P., 12
Kuwait, 7

Lachs, Thomas, 50
LAFTA (Latin American Free

Trade Association), 13
Lall, Sanjaya, 17
Libya, 89
Linder, Staffan Burenstam, 95, 97
Linnemann, Hans, 94
location advantage, 73-8
Lomé Convention, 142
London, 8
Luxembourg, 127

Mediterranean, 8, 142
MFN (most favoured nation)
    treatment, 52, 65, 118, 121, 135,
    140, 142
Middle East, 12, 117, 125, 143
Monnet, Jean, 127
Montesquieu, 11
Morgenthau, Hans J., 11
multinational enterprise, 8, 12, 74-6

Negev, 45
neighbouring countries, 9, 26, 53,
    65, 71, 81, 87, 88, 89, 92, 95, 97,
    103-5, 122-3, 135
Netherlands, 89, 91, 127
Nile, 44-5, 123
North-South, 15, 87
Nye, Joseph S., 12-14

OECD (Organisation for Economic
    Cooperation and
    Development), 97
Olson, Mancur, 50
OPEC (Organisation of Petroleum
    Exporting Countries), 15, 29
output creation, 53, 59-62, 71-2, 79,
    81, 88, 103, 138
ownership advantage, 73-8

Pacific, 142

Palestinian question, 136
Paris, Treaty of, 127
past
    belligerent(s), 9, 23, 47, 50-3,
        63-6, 71, 76, 79-82
    enemy, 34
Peace Treaty, Egyptian-Israeli, 118,
    121, 137
potential
    demand, 94, 96
    supply, 94, 96
    trade, 87-8, 114
preference agreement, 135
preferential trade, 120-2, 124-5
Prisoner's Dilemma, 4
probability of dissociation, 38-43,
    79, 80
producer interests, 50

Rapoport, Anatol, 145
recent
    belligerent(s), 7-9, 20, 23-4, 34,
        43, 47, 49, 67, 71, 77, 81-2, 87-8,
        126, 144-5
    enemy, 24, 67, 71
resistance to trade, 94-6, 100-3
risk of dissociation, 39, 82
Rom, Joseph, 5.

Sadat, Anwar, 3
Saudi Arabia, 7, 29
Schattschneider, Eimer E., 50
Schuman Plan, 127
Schuman, Robert, 144
sectoral approach, 126, 128, 132
Sinai, 5, 136-7
SITC (Standard International Trade
    Classification), 90, 94, 97, 104,
    107-11, 130
Soviet Union, 8, 12-13, 127

Sudan, 89
Suez Canal, 138
Switzerland, 8, 89-91
system
   exchange, 4, 145
   integrative, 4, 145
   threat, 4, 5, 145

third party, 76-82
Third World, 122
threat system, see system
trade
   agreement, 118, 120-2, 131, 139, 140
   balance, 137-8
   barrier(s), 53, 106, 120, 129-31, 141
   cooperation, 121-2
   creation, 50, 124-5
   diversion, 51, 81, 88, 105-9,
      113-15, 124-5
   expansion, 71, 95, 106, 108-15
   investment-related, 138, 139
trilateral
   cooperation, 143
   ventures, 77-81

UNCTAD (United Nations
   Conference on Trade and
   Development), 122
United Kingdom, 89, 127
United States, 5, 8, 11, 14, 127, 131, 141

Versailles Peace Treaty, 3
vested interest in peace, 47, 48,
   49-53, 60-5, 144
Vietnam, 12

Westphalia, 11